June Duncan Owen began writing as a child on the family vineyard, near Wentworth in far-western New South Wales; she sold her work early - she swapped bedtime stories for having her chores done by other children in the family. After graduating from the University of Adelaide, she became a social worker and teacher, married, and during years of moving to Singapore, Stawell, Adelaide, Canberra, and Hobart, with four children, found that bedtime storytelling was still important.

After finishing an Arts degree at the University of Tasmania, June became a working farmer, and then an antique dealer; she wrote articles and short stories for newspapers and magazines, and completed a Master's degree in history at the University of Sydney.

June is the author of *The Heart of the City* (a history of the Sydney City Mission) and a past president of the Society of Women Writers NSW Inc. She has taught writing and public speaking in courses, seminars, workshops for many years at places such as The University of New South Wales Union, University of Sydney Students' Union and The Australian Museum and on cruise ships. As well as writing, she speaks about Australian society, culture, & history and currently teaches writing at the Sydney WEA.

Writing & Selling Articles

JUNE DUNCAN OWEN

HALE
& IREMONGER

This edition
10 9 8 7 6 5 4 3 2 1

Printed and bound by
Australian Print Group Pty Ltd
Maryborough, Victoria

For the publisher
Hale & Iremonger Pty Ltd
GPO Box 2552, Sydney, NSW

National Library of Australia
Cataloguing-in-Publication

Owen, June Duncan.
Australian/New Zealand guide to writing and selling articles.

Rev. ed.
Bibliography.
Includes index.
ISBN 0 86806 621 4.

1. Authorship. 2. English language – Rhetoric. 3. Authorship – Marketing. 4. Authors and publishers – Australia. 5. Authors and publishers – New Zealand. I. Owen, June Duncan. How to write and sell articles. II.Title. III. Title: How to write and sell articles.

808.02

This book was previously published as *How to Write and Sell Articles* by Penguin Books Australia in 1992.

CONTENTS

Acknowledgements

Heartfelt thanks to my many students for questions, examples and unbounded enthusiasm; to Beryl Hill for encouragement and sympathetic, skilled editing; and most of all to Joshua for generous support and time, irreplaceable time.

1

DO YOU REALLY WANT TO WRITE?

WHY ARE YOU READING THIS BOOK?

'Writing is an adventure. To begin with, it is a toy and an amusement. Then it becomes a mistress, then it becomes a master, then it becomes a tyrant. The last phase is that just as you are about to become reconciled to your servitude, you kill the monster and fling him to the public.' *Winston Churchill*

Are you bursting with enthusiasm to express yourself in print? Do you want to learn a few techniques to help you express yourself more eloquently? Are you a born writer, if only you could get started? Do you wish to write, but have not yet had the confidence to try? Or do you have drawers full of material that has flowed effortlessly onto the page, but lack the confidence or the knowledge to submit it to an editor's scrutiny? Have you tried bravely to have your work published, but without success? Have you written, and perhaps even published, poetry or short stories in low-paying markets, and now wish to master non-fiction in order to increase your writing income?

No matter what your reason, any of these, or innumerable others, I hope using this book will enable you to join the band of writers whose work appears regularly in magazines and newspapers. Students taking my longer writing course often write their first article and have it accepted for publication during the course.

For the last ten years I have taught courses in writing articles and non-fiction in various educational and vocational institutions, writing societies, business houses, community groups in Australia and overseas. I currently teach regular courses in article writing and longer courses in non-fiction at the Workers' Educational Association, Sydney.

I will share with you the ideas and suggestions, the tips and techniques, that I share with my students; to the best of my ability I anticipate the questions that you might want to ask.

Most of all, I encourage you to have faith in yourself, faith that you can achieve whatever you want to achieve, if you take one step at a time. Other people have done it; so can you.

Producing good, readable, saleable, publishable non-fiction is partly a craft (a skill to be learned), partly an art, and partly a matter of learning to use our whole selves - brains and senses - in the most useful way. The techniques and the step-by-step process of mastering a craft can be *taught*; the art - the feel, the texture, the rhythm - needs closer attention and is usually instinctive, or caught from studying and learning from a master-model; better use of ourselves comes when we become more aware of how we function as writers.

There is nothing really special about writing as a skill. Many people have the talent, and I am sure you do, too, or you would not be reading this book. However, talent alone is not enough. You have to develop the skill, hone the craft, too. But if you have an eye for accuracy and detail, a curious mind, common sense, and a love of the English language, you can learn how to write successfully for the available magazine and newspaper markets.

DO YOU KNOW WHY YOU WANT TO WRITE?

Only when you know *why* you want to write will you know whether reading this book, or any other, will help you to reach your goal.

If you really want to write and publish good non-fiction, you will strive to write better and better articles. You will spread yourself to different kinds of non-fiction, to essays, travel writing, history, and reviews, or maybe you will move on to writing a regular column or to a staff position with a magazine. Or, going another step in the same direction, you might also begin writing book-length non-fiction.

Do you want to write articles because you think they are easier? Because you have heard they are better paid? Because you feel your talent is for factual writing? Because you have ideas you want to disseminate? Because you haven't found out yet where your writing strength lies, and you think non-fiction is a good place to start? All these reasons are valid. So are countless others. But I urge you to think about it for a while. Think about it until you know why you want to write.

Perhaps the only thing you are sure about is that you want to write. You may not be sure whether you really like non-fiction best, or fiction, or maybe plays or poetry. That's all right, too. Begin now, with the help of this book, to write and sell short pieces of non-fiction. Then, when you are selling your articles regularly, try writing a short story or a play. Do your best, but don't worry if your first effort in fiction doesn't sell straight away. After you have polished and pondered, send it out again (you will have learned some useful marketing tips for selling all manner of literary work from this book), but once you have sent it out, put it from your mind. Go back to writing articles. Get more success under your belt before you try writing more fiction. The first short story you sell might well be to one of the magazines which bought your non-fiction stories.

PRACTICE LEADS TO PUBLICATION

If you want to be a writer, you must write. Just knowing that you can write doesn't make you a writer. You become a writer *only* by writing – and you are a writer if you write, whether you are published or not. Some of the best-known authors wrote for ten years or more before they were published. By choosing to write articles for publication, you will not have to endure that time-lag.

Writing is one of those activities, like playing the piano, that improves with practise. But, unlike playing the piano, you don't have to share it with the world until you are ready to do so. If you are afraid that your nearest-and-dearest will laugh at your efforts, don't show them what you are doing. Write in secret if you must. Write every day if you can. Even a page a day, revised and edited and improved upon, will eventually produce good saleable work.

Writing is not one of those things you can put off doing until you are more skilful. You will only become more skilful by writing. First, you must *begin*. Then, if you write enough, and study enough, you have every chance of becoming a good writer.

Good writing, saleable writing, can be learned. Most of us have imaginative thoughts, a love of language, and a desire to communicate. Most of us need to think long and practise regularly before writing successfully for publication. A few lucky people write well immediately, and editors scramble for their work. Whichever category you are in, you can be a successful non-fiction writer. There is more than one road to the pot of gold

Though writing can be learned, I am not sure whether it can be taught. In my classes I discuss the range of possibilities and the ways that are usually most successful. I urge students to build on their own interests, feelings and experience. While I share tips and techniques that have worked for me and others, the success of my students comes as much from their own skills, desires and inner drives, as from following my guidelines.

Perhaps I just enable them to *act* on their long-held desires. Many students tell me that becoming aware of the different functions of the left and right sides of the brain (see Chapter 6), and then consciously separating their left- and right-brain activities, is the single most important technique they learn to apply. They also say that our discussions force them to become more aware of themselves, their world and the language with which they can most clearly describe that world, and that studying the available markets make them write more consciously for specific readers. I hope that this book will do the same for you.

When you write regularly, even if at first it is only for your own eyes, you will become an active learner again. The passivity induced by being no more than a watcher of life and/or television will vanish. Writing will help you to know and understand your material and your world - and yourself. The old adage - 'I hear and I forget, I see and I remember, I do and I understand' - becomes real for a writer.

In writing you are forced to be precise. Before you can communicate clearly with the reader, you must be absolutely clear about your material. You must know what you want to say. As you choose the precise word to clarify a thought, as you shape a paragraph to communicate an idea, the subject matter becomes clear to you. Only then can you transmit your thoughts clearly to your readers.

DO YOU HAVE WHAT IT TAKES?

I have already said that most people who want to write have enough talent to write successfully. It is not lack of talent that causes some beginners to hesitate so long that they never actually begin. There are a few other assets you must have, or be willing to develop:

- You must be aware. You must have sensitive antennae to tune into the world as it changes. You must be an observer. It helps if you also enjoy the foibles of our society and our world.

- You must love words, and have a strong desire to communicate in words.

- You must be creative and imaginative. Even for the most factual of writing you need to see connections, and foresee effects.

- You must have confidence in yourself, and in the worth of what you have to say. You must trust your own good taste and judgement.

- You must develop the discipline to write regularly, even when you are tired, even when you don't feel like it.

- You must value yourself and your work enough to sometimes choose writing over other activities. This may mean that you lose some friends or perhaps upset your family. You must take your work seriously, before you can expect anyone else to do so.

- You must develop a professional attitude. This means you have to be tough enough to collect rejections from the letter-box, and post your work out again. It is your work that, for one reason or another, is being rejected, *not you.*

- You must have had some experience of life, before you can write. Don't stop living to write. It doesn't work that way. You must have something to say. No matter what your age, you must know what you are writing about, either from experience or research.

- It helps if you have good health and stamina.

Nine assets! If you don't have them, you can develop them. But the tenth asset is the most important of all. It glimmers through several of the points above, but it deserves a separate paragraph. Without it, the other nine assets don't count. This most vital attribute of all is perhaps the hardest one for a writer to develop, and it needs to be constantly worked on. No matter how long you have been writing successfully, this asset will still need to be stroked, nurtured, encouraged. It is the key to success for every writer. Hold it fast; write it out in large letters and stick it above your keyboard or desk, on your mirror, on the refrigerator door. Never let your consciousness of its importance slip!

- ***You must have faith in yourself and faith in your writing.*** Even when you are just beginning you must feel that what you are writing is worthwhile. It may perhaps not be as good as you hope it will be after a little practice, a little training. You know that with practice you will get better and better, not worse and worse. But, for now, your work is as good as you can make it.

  When friends and acquaintances comment that you seem to have dropped out of the social round, tell them why. Say proudly that you have just finished an article on, say, the way children in boarding schools develop independence early. Some won't be interested, but some will. If the latter ask where it will be appearing, put on your most confident look and say, 'I hope it will appear in the *XYZ Journal of Christian Education.*'

  If you are asked at a high-powered dinner party, or a chat session at the cricket or tennis club, what you do, never mumble, 'Well, I just scribble a little.' Instead, with your head held high, say clearly, 'I write.' And, there is no need to add that until you establish yourself you also sell hamburgers to pay the bills. Who knows, there might be an editor, or an editor's cousin, in the group. Almost as good, there may be another writer with whom you can share tips and local information.

  Though writers tend to be very private people as a rule, it is worth the effort to 'make an effort'. Those writers who take any available opportunity to sell themselves almost invariably sell their work too, and usually at a higher price. When you think about why you want to write, you will realise that your only irreplaceable asset is yourself, your own unique identity. There is no one else quite like you in the whole world. There never has been and there never will be. No one else will ever have the world view that you have; no one else will express themselves as you do. You are a one-off - flaunt it!

- By writing articles you are in the best possible position to make a success of your writing. Factual material outsells fiction everywhere - in books, magazines, and of course, in newspapers. Non-fiction writers, therefore, have a more open market-place. If you have been trying to become a published writer, you have a much better chance with non-fiction.

  The reason may be that readers everywhere are more interested in an identifiable speaker or writer. They want to read what *you* have to say. Since everyone is different, everyone has something different to say, and a different way of saying it. If you feel hesitant, and feel that you can not give your opinion yet, then start with fully researched articles (see Chapter 7).

GETTING TO KNOW YOURSELF

Please take time to think now. Do you really want to write, rather than do something else? You may have the talent, but then talent alone is not so rare. Writing takes time, and the life-span of all of us is limited. Do you want to spend your life writing? Or doing something else? You almost certainly have other talents - would you enjoy exercising them even more? Overnight success in any segment of the literary world is rare. The authors you hear of whose first book was a best-seller almost certainly have been writing for ten years and have two or three earlier books stowed away in a bottom drawer, or consigned to the waste-paper basket.

For now, give some thought as to whether you want to spend your life writing. I did not ask whether you want to *be* a writer. That is a vastly different question. But you can't be a writer without writing. Writing is a lonely occupation; it is very demanding, and rarely as well paid as other intellectual professions. At first most people have to write part-time while they earn money in some other manner.

If you really want to write, if you have an unstoppable urge to communicate your thoughts and feelings, if you have something to say that you want to share with others, no profession is more varied, more interesting, more free. If you are prepared to give of yourself, no profession is more rewarding.

I believe, with Thomas Carlyle, that the character of the writer must lie recorded in everything that is written. Is there anything you feel passionately about? If so, then that is where you should start writing, for writing is not only about words, about structure, about ideas, about marketing; writing is about passion.

Writing is your way of communicating with the world. More people will read your writing than you will ever meet. So communicate what you care about, what is important to you.

To succeed in this business of writing it is important that you believe in yourself and your ultimate ability to succeed. It doesn't matter if your general education has been inadequate. Most adults have learned more out of school than in, no matter how long or formal that schooling was.

It doesn't matter that you feel you have spent too many years in a dead-end job. From now on you will have a second, vitally interesting job. Besides, your work experiences provide situations and characters you can use as material in your writing.

It doesn't matter if your duties to your family take almost all your time and strength. If your family is discouraging, you can use them as material for your stories - disguised, of course.

It doesn't matter whether you are in your teens or whether you are past retirement age - no editor I know has ever asked the age of contributors.

If you want to write, you will write. I hope I will be able to help you to make a success of it.

TAKE TIME, AND BE KIND TO YOURSELF

Your mind, your imagination, and your ideas are your primary resource. Take the time to think about how accepting the challenge of becoming a writer might change your life. You will have to initiate some of the changes, some of them will come unbidden.

I will assume that you expect to enjoy your life as a professional writer; why else would you want to do it? When you begin to take writing seriously you step onto a wheel, or, more properly, a spiral: writing regularly with confidence will mean more production, which will bring sales and success, which will boost your confidence to write more, and so on.

The beginning writer often starts to write too soon. Think about the sorts of writing and the subjects which will come easily to you. Give yourself time to develop a positive attitude. To establish a regular discipline of writing, and that is necessary to become prolific, you must first develop a confident, happy approach to the whole business of devoting part of your day to writing. Besides, it's more fun. If you are going to spend a large part of your life writing, then it is important that it is fun.

Believe in your ideas; believe in what you are doing. Give yourself encouragement, not discouragement. Give yourself rewards, not punishment. Do things the easy way, not the hard way. Protect yourself from knockers, from interruptions during your precious writing time, and avoid people who depress you. Don't set impossible deadlines; that is asking for failure.

Each chapter of this book will help you to work through and master the various steps in producing readable, and thus saleable, writing. Along with the practical tips and techniques, examples and exercises, and shared knowledge of the publishing world, I will take you to a stage where you are in control of more intangible matters that will concern you as a writer.

As you write you will encounter many issues which you must square with your own conscience. These will range from the simple travel article which you have arranged to sell before setting off for your holiday. But you find the resort overpriced and not nearly as good a destination as others you have enjoyed. Do you write the piece anyway, praising what you can? Or do you contact the magazine and tell the editor that you will not be able to supply the article? Or is there a third way?

You may initially be interested in, and anxious to publicise, the success of a scheme to establish small groups of intellectually disabled adults in ordinary suburban houses. On the one hand, you believe that this is a marvellous improvement on the old hostel-type of 'home' and you think the forward-looking social workers should be commended for helping such people fit into the community. On the other hand, your article might draw attention to such houses - make them seem different in some way - and that would certainly be counterproductive to the efforts of social workers and the people trying to fit in unobtrusively.

Exercises

1 Read dozens of newspapers and magazines. The magazines and papers of most interest to you, and most likely to hold articles of the kind you want to write, will be the ones you read regularly. But don't restrict yourself to these. Range widely, borrowing and buying journals with which you are not familiar - as long as they look interesting. Try for a broad sweep, including weekly and monthly news, travel, general-interest magazines, as well as special-interest magazines such as business, arts, sporting, men's and women's magazines; don't neglect trade journals, including those which are sent only to subscribers. Check with your family and friends, your doctor, accountant, etc., and borrow their professional journals.

Spend time on this. Read, read, read.

2 Put aside the articles you particularly like. Go through this pile, and mark those articles most nearly resembling the kind of article you would like to write. There will be a mixture, of course. If you have wide interests, then a wide variety of articles will appeal to you.

As you read and study each one, turn to the panel, usually on the second or third page in magazines, which lists the staff (starting from the editor right through to the advertising assistant), and check whether your chosen articles are staff-written. Some magazines and newspapers list only senior editorial staff, so if the writer is not identified as a staff member, look further. Check the contents page to see if the topics of your chosen articles are included as regular features. Several articles by the same writer in the same issue also suggests that they are staff-written. Magazines will always print work by a staff-writer, even if they receive a better submission from a freelance writer. The reason is clear: the staff-writer is already on the pay-roll. If you suspect the article is staff-written, discard it. You are looking for an opening for a freelance writer.

3 Read, reread, and select at least ten articles of the kind that you would like to write now. You are not looking for the pinnacle of your success

as a writer, but neither should you choose something you would not be proud to have written. Choose articles which engage your interest, which you enjoy reading, which, with a little help, *you* could write.

2

WHAT TO WRITE ABOUT

'You don't write because you want to say something; you write because you've got something to say' —F. Scott Fitzgerald

In this chapter we will go, step by step, through ways to think about, and how to decide upon, what to write about; how to get ideas and how to use them; how to choose the best topic; and how to focus your article.

What can you write best about? The classic advice for all writers is to write about what you know. Most beginning writers start by writing about their own experiences. This is good practice. Take care that familiarity has not blunted your perceptions.

LEARN TO OBSERVE

To write well, you must first *see* clearly, with your eyes and your mind. Sometimes this means you have to walk around a subject, literally or figuratively, and look at it from all angles, until you are confident that you perceive it as it is.

A few years ago, hunting for my great-grandfather's former home, Warrakoo, in Wareham, England, I found what I thought was the right house. However, it had a different name emblazoned over its door. It was all shut up, the occupants obviously absent, so I followed up my next lead, the parish church. The ancient verger, when I asked him if he could show me where Warrakoo was, greeted me like a long-lost cousin.

'I certainly can,' he said, 'I've walked or ridden my bicycle past that house every day for the past eighty years. I passed it on my way to school, and now I pass it on my way to the church!' We walked there together, the verger pushing his bicycle. 'There it is,' he swept his arm in a grand gesture, 'and it hasn't changed at all in the eighty years I've known it.'

I pointed to the name above the door. The verger was astounded, and reacted as if a trick had been played upon him. We were joined by neighbours then, so he asked them when Warrakoo's name had been changed. Several of the neighbours conferred for a couple of minutes, and then informed us that the name had been changed when the present owners purchased the house in 1939. The verger had passed the house twice daily for fifty years, without noticing that its clearly emblazoned name had been changed since the days of his youth.

Don't be a shut-in. Go out, and look at and listen to life around you. But *really* look, don't wear blinkers, and *really* listen - even if it sometimes means unobtrusive eavesdropping.

As a writer you will become a professional observer; you will learn to concentrate; you will learn to analyse. Everything you see, hear, smell, taste, and touch, will be truly perceived. So automatic will this become that you will feel that your senses have become sharper. You will become more aware. From now on, you will see all your daily experiences, all the things and people that surround you in your daily life, as material that might be used in an article.

As you gather impressions and observations, you will form opinions on all sorts of things that formerly did not engage your interest - all the better if you become passionately involved. You will write more strongly about those things that you care about; if you care, your readers will care.

LEARN TO QUESTION

Instead of just perceiving what is happening, find out *why* it is happening. Your story will have more depth if you know not only what is, but why it is. People are always most interested in other people, so *who* is involved is important. The *where, when* and *how* make your story specific and immediate. Whatever you write about, ask and answer all your readers' questions - before they ask them.

LEARN TO TAKE NOTES

You only have to listen to two people giving sworn evidence about an accident they both witnessed to realise how imperfect our memories are. By concentrating on what you observe, your ability to recall it in detail will improve. But all of us are fallible. So when you feel you are likely to write about a subject - an event, a thing, a person, an experience - take notes.

Many writers keep a notebook and write in it daily. If that seems a chore, remember that all writing is practice. How marvellous it is, when you are trying to think of how to describe something in words that will evoke a clear mental picture, to be able to turn to your notebook and read your own on-the-spot description.

Take notes, not only of the things you see and do but of what you hear, smell, feel, and think. Even if you never reread the notes you make, they are yours. You are more likely to recall that experience, even the words you used to describe it, if you have already expressed the image, the impression or the thought in words, and written them down.

KEEP UP TO DATE

The world changes. Make sure it does not leave you behind. This does not mean that you must dress your writing in modern jargon, nor does it mean you must embrace all change with glee. But you must know about the changes occurring. Even if you write deploring the way the modern world turns, your article will be more authoritative, and thus more convincing, if you are aware of the different aspects of the changes - the causes, how different people are affected - the good points as well as the bad.

HOW TO GET IDEAS

Most writers have more ideas than they could use in seven lifetimes. But I have been asked too often where I get my ideas to skim lightly over this aspect. Besides, we all have blank days when we would beg, borrow, or even steal, a good idea.

Ideas, by the way, are like the air, free. They cannot be copyrighted. It is what you do with the idea, how you express it, that becomes your saleable property. An idea can begin with any of the following.

- Something you see - you become more than a reporter, you look for the less obvious characteristics and details of a person or place; you learn to truly see afresh, with your eyes, and not what your mind expects that you will see.

- A thought, or a word overheard in a conversation - talk to people (the taxi-driver, the plumber), ask questions.

- A dream which you note down in the morning before you forget it.

- A passion or something you care deeply, and probably

know a lot, about - this might lead to many articles which will perhaps need to be focused narrowly, and may well lead to a non-fiction book - you could become known as a specialist in that topic.

- Your reading will often spark a related, or even opposing, idea - daily newspapers are a mine of ideas. Subjects which a journalist mentions only briefly, can, with a little research, become full-length articles. Radio and television news, and, in particular, current affairs programs, very often glance at topics begging for further investigation and expansion into an article. Visit libraries, browse in bookshops.

- Your family and your neighbours - did they have a problem; was it solved or not? If it interested you, it may well interest others.

- An interesting event in your locality - if the newly-elected member of parliament or newly-promoted town clerk comes from another city, another state, then it is likely that you could sell an article about the current minor celebrity to the home-town newspaper.

- Your daily work - if you work at a check-out counter, or in a fast-food outlet, write of the people you see there and of their foibles; if you have the full-time care of small children, use their view of the world. A bus driver sees a cross-section of the community every day. Everyone who spends time in public places, either as a worker or as an observer, will notice idiosyncrasies among the people passing by that will amuse readers. It is no coincidence that many of the best writers have practised medicine; they have learnt to observe people.

- Lectures, sermons, specialist and professional journals, company reports - you may have the knowledge and the skill to turn a specialist subject into one of general appeal.

- Interesting moments, startling scenes, and mini-character sketches, which would make a filler, or a longer article - it is really a matter of becoming aware, of putting out your antennae, and being sensitive to what is happening around you.

- Draw deliberately on your memory; day-dream with a purpose - this works best if you try to remember in finest detail a particular time or incident in your life. Distance in time often lends balance, objectivity, sometimes a whimsical nostalgia. Did you grow up in the country? the inner city? in a lighthouse off the coast? Were you an only child - and lonely? the eldest of twelve? Were you educated by correspondence, by a governess/tutor? at a one-teacher school? at a now-defunct boarding school? in a school which now has a well-known reputation - for any reason? Were you married young? jilted at the church? Did your child have a rare disease? survive a spectacular accident? save your sanity? or your life?

- Above all, write articles about *people* - things people do, invent, suffer; things that happen to people; how scientific or technical developments or inventions affect people; the people who live in a particular city or country, how their lives differ from the average, the humdrum, etc. Travel means going to a different place, and your holiday trips can spawn ideas for articles. The core that lies behind the varying themes of most travel articles is either the people of that place, or how that place will affect people like your readers.

THE RIGHT IDEA TO WRITE ABOUT NOW

This, too, is a very personal thing. In fact, all through this book, I will tell you that you must do what suits you. Writing is a very personal activity. That is one of its charms. When I tell you what works for me or other writers I know, I hope you will use that tip as you see fit. Try my method if you like, until you develop another that suits you better. Or treat it with disdain, and throw it out straight away.

Even if you follow my suggestions exactly you will never write what I would write in the way I would write it. Just as I could never write as you do. We each learn to write with our own voice. The best part is that the voice changes with our mood and our experience.

So, what article idea should you choose? My choice would be:

- The big idea, the idea that matters! An idea that could change the world, or at least a significant part of society.

- The idea that you care about, even if it is not widely known. If it matters to you your passion will show, and it is likely to evoke interest, even passion, in others. Often a story about an individual will convey a universal truth very effectively. A story about a physically handicapped person who is successful will make the point in an interesting way that we are more than our physical bodies.

- The idea that seems timely now. But don't forget that the lead-time of a weekly magazine is often six weeks, of a monthly sometimes six months.

- An idea that is relevant to many people, one an editor would see as being of interest to many readers.

- An idea that seems to have a completeness, a unity, so that it seems to be asking to be told. Perhaps one that expresses a universal truth vividly and without the preachy tone of a proverb.

- An idea that appeals to the self-interest of many readers. This covers a wide range, and includes aspects of all the basic needs of humanity, as well as many of the wants and desires, such as: hunger and thirst (anything on food, nutrition, wines, etc.), shelter (all aspects of homes, gardens, holidays, etc.), acquisitiveness (all kinds of investment, home ownership, earnings in various professions, fashion, cars, etc.), self-preservation (medical advice or news, pop-psychology, keep-fit, safe-driving tips, self-defence, or dangers, disasters, fires, wars, etc.), self-improvement (education, how to be successful, how to help children do better at school, etc.), recreation, including sport. If you seek out ideas that directly or indirectly cater to your readers' self-interests, you will succeed in selling your articles. (A word of warning: we are all readers, so never adopt an air of superiority as an author.)

- People are interested, firstly, in themselves and, next, in other people, particularly if they can identify with them or relate to them in some way, or learn from their experience. What are called 'service pieces' are articles with information that serves the reader. These are among the easiest to sell of all articles. All general-interest magazines have a high proportion of service pieces, though they may not all be labelled as 'How-to's'. They may include such topics as 'Make money on real estate despite high interest-rates'; 'Remain sane while raising five teenagers'; 'Nappy-rash-proof your baby'.

- Many people are interested in helping others. If you want to write for them, then seek out the journals directed at that market.

- Above all, you must write on topics which interest you. If your interests are wide, so much the better. The more topics you enjoy writing about, the more markets will be open to you.

FOCUS YOUR IDEAS

Ideas may be born in a flash of insight, but then they must be focused and fashioned to fit the needs of a particular magazine.

Many ideas first suggest topics or subjects that are too broad or general to be satisfactorily dealt with in an article. They need to be narrowed, focused so just one aspect is followed up, one point made. Travel-writer Jan Morris, who usually writes very long articles, decides what particular aspect of a place she will cover, even before she goes there. The late Ian Mudie, a prolific Australian writer and teacher, told me what he saw as the difference between a novel and a short story - a novel is written as if one is sitting on a balcony overlooking the world, while a short story is written as if one is standing on tiptoe peering through a small window into a lighted room.

An article, too, is a self-contained piece of writing that loses its effectiveness if the view is broad rather than concentrated. Don't try to write an article about Sydney. The subject is too big to be adequately covered in an article. Instead write on, say, the work of lifesavers at Sydney's beaches. Don't write about a trip to Egypt, but about a trip down the Nile, or even about the various boats on which tourists can sail down the Nile. Don't write an article on Los Angeles, but on the Mexican bars in Alveira Street. By concentrating on one point, you are able to get close enough to a subject to go into precise and intimate detail, details which are likely to be new and interesting to many of your readers. In short, when looking at a subject or idea for an article, use a microscope rather than a telescope.

Some subjects are already so inherently narrow that to awaken reader-interest it is necessary to relate them to the wider world. Many science subjects only become interesting for general readers if the knowledgeable writer can relate them to everyday life.

A technique I use in my classes to expand ideas and to decide on a suitable focus, is based on an adaptation of a

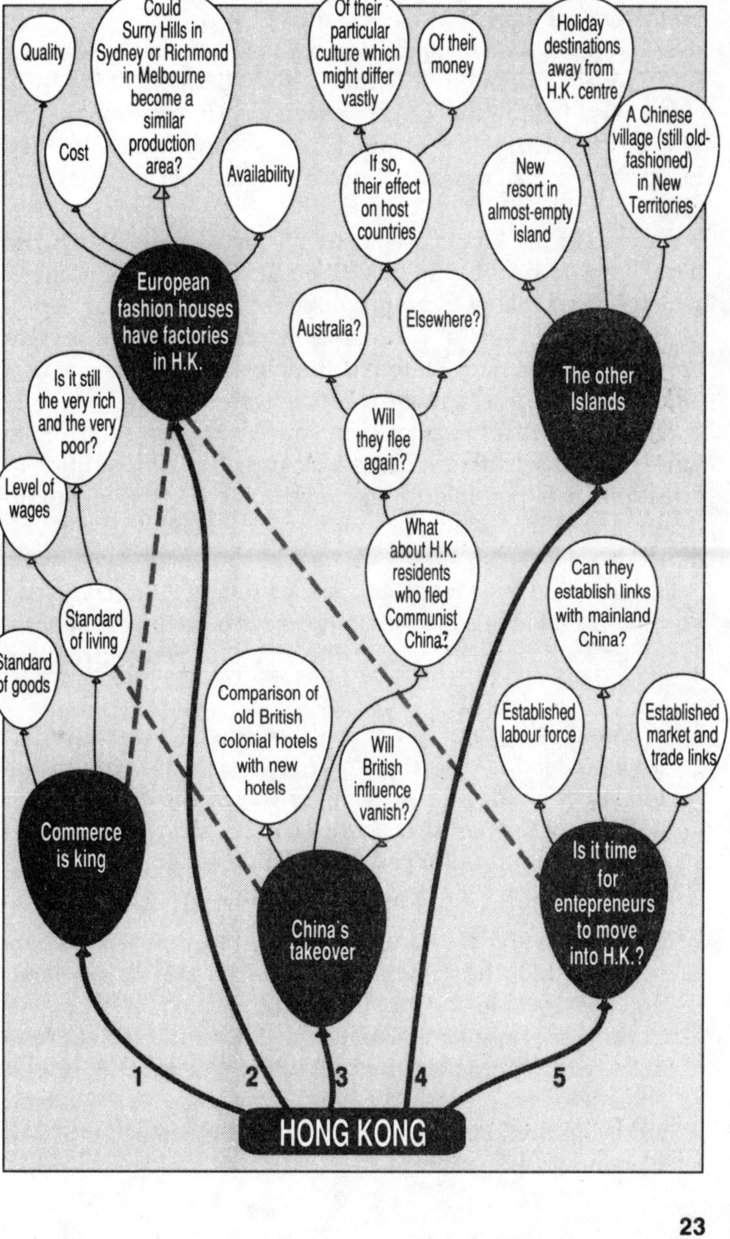
HONG KONG
1
2
3
4
5
Commerce is king
Standard of goods
Standard of living
Level of wages
Is it still the very rich and the very poor?
European fashion houses have factories in H.K.
Quality
Cost
Could Surry Hills in Sydney or Richmond in Melbourne become a similar production area?
Availability
China's takeover
Comparison of old British colonial hotels with new hotels
Will British influence vanish?
What about H.K. residents who fled Communist China?
Will they flee again?
Australia?
Elsewhere?
If so, their effect on host countries
Of their particular culture which might differ vastly
Of their money
The other Islands
New resort in almost-empty island
Holiday destinations away from H.K. centre
A Chinese village (still old-fashioned) in New Territories
Is it time for entepreneurs to move into H.K.?
Established labour force
Can they establish links with mainland China?
Established market and trade links

brainstorming idea that has been used widely. Many of you may have met the technique before in brainstorming sessions. I call my adaptation 'ballooning', mainly because each idea is circled and held to the 'trigger-word' by strings, and thus the whole affair looks like a bunch of balloons. I also like the image of 'up, up and away', which suits both balloons and ideas.

As you can see I have used 'Hong Kong' as the trigger-word here. It sprouted ideas in five different directions, any one of which I could follow to write a cohesive article on one aspect of this subject. It is also possible to make sensible bridges between two or more different bunches if they have logical links, as in this case, and if the article is to be a long one.

The main benefit of ballooning your ideas before starting to write the article is that it gives a clear picture of the different directions it is possible to take, and for a short to medium-length article it is almost always better to head firmly in one direction.

Each of these five ideas leads me in a different direction, and you could probably add at least five more bunches of balloons.

Let us look more closely at the five numbered strings of balloons.

1 'Commerce is king' is a much too general statement, but it would lead to consideration of two separate aspects: the quality of goods and the level of wages and the standard of living of the populace, both rich and poor. This is a self-contained group of ideas, and could lead to an article in itself. Or it could be linked to number 2.

2 This bunch of ideas sprang from the fact that several European fashion houses have set up factories in Kowloon. The designs and the labels, and often the fabrics, are all European – only the workmanship is Chinese. It could lead to an article comparing this area with the centre of Sydney's and Melbourne's and Auckland's rag trade. For a longer, more comprehensive article it could be linked with number 1 or number 5, or both.

3 The political direction would begin with Hong Kong's takeover by Communist China, and a tightly focused article could probably not take into account all the sprouted balloons. One balloon on the comparison of old colonial hotels with the new hardly seems to fit at all, and would certainly make an article on its own. Depending on your material and your interest, you could follow the likely change in the lives of those residents who will remain and those who will go (or have already gone) to other countries. You could write an overview – or concentrate on Australia or New Zealand or any other country as a destination. So already we have looked at four possible articles from this *one* balloon string. It is possible, too, that if we want to write more on a political/economics angle we could combine some of number 3 with number 1, and find another point of view for number 3 which could also be combined with number 5.

4 Rather than look at Hong Kong as a shopping-holiday destination, I looked away from that much covered subject to the other islands of the colony. A comprehensive article could cover all the subsidiary balloons on the number 4 string - or you could write a more intimate, detailed article on any one of them if you had experienced them and observed closely.

5 This could make a 'new ideas/investment' type of article for a publisher with a strong readership of adventurous investors, or for hands-on small investors and business people. It might also find a home in a fashion trade journal (as, of course, number 2 would too).

SAVE IDEAS FOR A RAINY DAY

I do not mean that you should hoard ideas as if they were a scarce commodity. On the contrary, I like to use ideas rashly, spending ideas with profligacy such as I have never been able to enjoy with money. I believe that the spending of ideas initiates more, many more. It's like priming the pump.

In the sense that ideas are likely to take you unawares, to flash by if you are not watching, then writers need to develop a method of snaring them, and pinning them down for later use. Don't let them escape! Write them down. Fully-fledged ideas can be filed methodically (more of that later in Chapter 11), but it is important to capture and nurture the merest hint or germ of an idea.

The best method of dealing with the germ of an idea is to let your unconscious mind work on it. But if your unconscious mind is like mine, it will need constant reminding. So write your germ of an idea in the middle of a large sheet of paper and tape it on the wall above your desk, on your wardrobe door, on the back of the bathroom door, or on the refrigerator. As your mind comes up with data to turn it into a complete idea, add those snippets of ideas, anecdotes, information or evidence to the notes you have already jotted down. At this point you might do the ballooning exercise. When you feel happy that there is now enough information for you to work on in due course, file it in an ideas file (see Chapter 11).

When you read the daily paper, clip items of interest. Add them to the file, either as ideas to follow up, or as supporting material for ideas you have already filed. When your ideas file is bulging, sort it into categories of your different interests, or file the ideas in alphabetical order. Work out some way that suits you. The important thing is that you know where to find something you have filed. Go through your ideas file occasionally, so that you know exactly what you have, otherwise possible subjects may lie there until they are out of date.

You might find helpful an outline of the method I use. But use it as a starting point, and fit it to your needs. Everyone works differently, and as you develop into a professional (even if only part-time) working writer you will develop a system that is right for your method of working, your storage facilities, etc. (for more detail on this, see Chapter 11).

This is what I currently do, because I now have a large study which is strictly off-limits to everyone else. I know if I leave something on my desk for further attention, it will be there tomorrow, next week or next month. You could try adapting my routine to suit your circumstances.

- When I get a likely idea (after it has passed the clipping-to-the-refrigerator-door stage, and it really does seem not only possible, but interesting), I write the subject clearly on a manila folder, and file it alphabetically. As time goes by, I add newspaper cuttings, references, possible anecdotes, quotations or any other related ideas I come across or which occur to me - all these go into the folder. This gestation period may take weeks or months, depending on whether the subject will date, or how many other projects I have on the go.

- When I am ready to work actively on that idea (that is, if I plan to begin writing in two or three weeks), I mark it clearly with a working title and a projected starting date, and either bring it to the front of the filing cabinet or onto my desk.

- From that time on I hold that idea in the 'second row' of my consciousness. Ideas, information, and illustrations, all come thick and fast *while I am finishing my current work.* I may make telephone enquiries and line up interviews for the coming work during this period. I almost certainly ask one or two editors if they are interested. Everything I do related to that project is noted, dated, and slipped into the file. When I am ready to begin, I often find that I have very little further research to do.

- It often happens that I have collected too widely and there is material I cannot use in this article. After deciding on the most suitable focus, and writing the article, I throw out any outdated material, and then I slip everything back into the file. It will continue to accumulate until I write another article from a slightly different angle or with a different emphasis for a different market.

FACT OR FICTION?

All writing coming from within yourself is creative, so do not feel that because you aim for the non-fiction market you are not creative. Writing a saleable article takes creativity, clarity of thought and language, craft (the writing skills), and marketing skills. These are exactly the same broad skills needed to become a successful novelist, poet, playwright or historian.

In article writing, fact is fact, so do try to separate in your own mind what is fact and what is non-fact. Don't 'colour' the facts; don't use 'almost-facts' or 'might-have-been-facts' as facts.

As a non-fiction writer, you are implicitly telling readers that what you write is true. The readers will believe you, unless you give them reason for doubting you. With editors your reputation will depend upon your accuracy, your integrity, and the reliability of your research. So check your facts, and then check them again.

Of course, I am aware, and you will be too, that the English language we use, however fastidiously, is so laden with meaning that it is frighteningly easy to imply opinions and judgements when supposedly stating bald facts. (For further discussion on this, see Chapter 5.)

Quotes must be exact if they are direct quotations. Even if they are paraphrases they must be true in intent; true to the spirit of what the speaker actually said. Some editors will insist upon knowing the full names and occupations of people quoted, so get their permission to be quoted. However, if it is a controversial article such as an exposé, you must have other evidence, such as a tape. Unless a scoop drops into your lap, it might be wiser for a beginner not to write a controversial article. Most editors would need to know you before accepting an article likely to attract a libel suit.

Yes, you can include your opinion, your views on the subject, but always make it clear that your views are just that - your views. All writing reveals the writer: the better the writing, the more it reveals. But it should not blatantly reveal the writer, nor is the best writing confessional - that is not only self-revealing but self-indulgent.

Your most successful writing will have humanity and warmth - and it will come when you are writing on a subject which grips you. Such writing is your way of telling the world something of what is important to you. It expresses your knowledge, your experience or authority, even your opinions, your feelings, your view of the world.

If you are enthusiastic about your subject, then you have a good chance of making your readers feel enthusiastic, too. But, remember, *all readers want to see some relevance to their own lives.*

Here is a simple check-list, to give your idea the best chance of being accepted.

Is it exciting?

Is it up-to-date?

Is it relevant to many people?

Is it the truth?

Is it fair?

Will it build good will?

Is it beneficial to someone?

Does it inform, instruct, inspire or entertain?

If it needs illustrations, have you provided them? Even if it can stand alone, would illustrations in the form of maps, diagrams, photographs or sketches improve the article?

If the subject is broad, have you narrowed it down, given it a specific focus?

Does it strike a balance between personal (subjective) and impersonal (objective) that is right for the topic and the market?

TO SPECIALISE OR NOT?

It depends on you. What makes you happy? Do you have an overriding interest in, and a better-than-average knowledge of, a broad subject which fascinates you? Or do you have a butterfly mind which enjoys briefly researching new ideas and new topics? Or a combination of the two?

It is certainly easier to write an article in the same or related field as one you have written before. If more research is needed you will know where to look, and thus you will be able to quickly gather together whatever is needed. If you know the subject, if you are qualified by training or experience, you will be able to write with authority, your credibility will be unquestioned.

There are other advantages, too. As you become known as a writer in your particular field, you may be asked to write a regular column, or you may be sought as a speaker. All these things will add to your income without much additional effort on your part.

There are few disadvantages, the most important being that you might become bored. It is true that the market for your specialty might collapse, but this is unlikely to happen in any of the major categories of subjects. If technology or the changing values of society did make your special subject obsolete, then it would probably be easy for you to up-date.

I cannot repeat too often that you should write about what interests you. Even if you are only interested in the life-cycle of Christmas beetles, there are many science magazines throughout the world to which you could sell; the subject could be simplified and written for the readers of general-interest magazines, women's magazines, men's magazines, gardening magazines, outdoor magazines, children's magazines. Even daily newspapers would be a likely market at that time each year when the beetles appear.

Most writers choose the middle road. They choose ten, twenty or thirty subjects in which they are particularly interested, and become specialists in all those areas. Or they choose, say, two very broad but related specialties, such as travel and eating out. As you can see, they overlap to a great degree; research could be combined, and yet there would be infinite variety.

Writers who have a specialist science background are lucky because they can often write with an authority that no amount of research can match. One of my students was a marine biologist whose working experience was mainly in recording the sounds made by dolphins, fish, and other reef and ocean creatures. A popular-science magazine paid better-than-average rates for his first article on the 'singing fish', and asked for more. His long-term plan was to explain marine science to general readers, and he was well on his way with his very first article.

So, will you specialise, or will you write about whatever strikes your fancy? If you write about what interests you, then your limits will be as broad as your interests. The more diverse your interests, the more markets will be open to you.

Exercises

1 Take the ten or more articles you have already put aside as specially appealing to you, and read them again. Browse over them, think about them, and at the top of each one write *in one sentence* what you believe the writer is saying in the article.

2 Select one article which is of the kind that you could most easily write without much further work, that is, without much further research. We are talking about the kind of article here, not the topic. For example, if a weekend paper prints a human-interest story about a five-year-old girl in the streets of Kings Cross (someone the readers can empathise with in an unexpected place), then the editor may also be interested in your story about your next-door neighbour who is a Polish countess working as a paper-seller! If you like fishing you might be able to write 'How to Catch Silver Perch in the Murray' along the lines of a published story in a fishing magazine.

Remember, look for the kind of article you feel you could write *now*. It is always better to try first something quite easy, and in length between 500 and 1500 words. Stretch your writing muscles gradually. Successful mountaineers first practise on small hills.

3 Put your chosen article centre-stage on your desk. Read it several times. Leave it there. Think briefly about the things you could write about. Do you regularly read the newspaper or magazine from which you selected your article? If so, then you are a typical reader. That should make it easy for you to recognise a topic that regular readers would enjoy reading about.

4 Imagine the article you could have had published instead of the chosen article (that is, one of a similar kind that, had the editor been able to see it), that *may* have been chosen instead of the one that was published. Do you have something to say that other people would want to hear? Be very clear about what it is you want to say to your readers.

5 Balloon your topic. See what related ideas you come up with. Decide on one direction to follow, one focus.

6 Make notes on your topic, information, anecdotes, or anything else that you think will help to shape your article. Put it in a folder and clearly mark the cover 'Article No. 1' (or a suitable working title) and add the date. Leave it on your desk or in some handy place so that you can add information as it occurs to you.

7 Write in one sentence exactly what you want to tell the reader of your proposed article.

3

WRITING THE ARTICLE

'Put it before them briefly so they will read it, clearly so they will appreciate it, picturesquely so they will remember it and, above all, accurately so they will be guided by its light' —Joseph Pulitzer

FROM BUILDING BLOCKS TO FINISHED STRUCTURE

The last chapter dealt with deciding what to write. We discussed the advantage of asking, 'What do I want to write?', instead of saying, 'I want to write'.

After you have selected a topic (as outlined in the Exercises), how do you go about writing a saleable article on that selected topic? There are many aspects to consider: the language used, the depth and tone of the piece, the effect you want to achieve, as well as the manner in which you say what you want to say. Writing, successful writing, depends upon the exactness with which the writer transfers the thought or the picture in his or her mind to the mind of the reader. The purity of that transfer depends upon the accurate use and arrangement of words. (The use of language, the importance of using words that mean the same thing, or as nearly as possible, to both the writer and the reader, the dangers of using value-laden language and other aspects of language use, are covered in Chapter 5.)

How can you arrange your material so that readers find it interesting, easy to follow and satisfying? The most logical ways of organising articles are the most successful and, therefore, the most common. They are easy to follow. Readers know where you are going - they won't lose their way.

PUBLIC vs PRIVATE WRITING

When you write in your diary, or notebook, the most careless arrangement of words or abbreviations of words and explanations will evoke the image or idea you want to remember. When you write to your family or people who know you well, know your values, share much of your experience, you can use a mutually understood 'shorthand', and be confident that they will know what you mean. That is private writing.

Public writing is different. Depending on how specific your audience is, you will have to make your meaning clear to a reader who does not share your mental world, who does not share your experience, education or understanding. Under these conditions you have to work harder to communicate with accuracy, to transfer your exact thought or mental picture to the mind of the reader.

DON'T MISS A STEP

You will need to take care that you do not lose your reader on the way. You know the subject (from personal experience or research), but the reader does not. If some of the links remain in your head, a reader trying to follow your thoughts may become bewildered, and stop reading. Check that there are no gaps in your information.

AVOID SIDE-TRACKS

An article must stand alone. You now know how important it is to narrow the focus and make one point, or to expound and elaborate on one clearly defined theme or thesis (see Chapter 2). Everything in the article must lead to or support your main idea. Don't put in titbits of extra evidence or fascinating anecdotes unless they add to or support that thesis. They will distract the readers, lead them away on side-tracks. Too many of these distractions, and you may well lose your readers altogether. If they do finish the article, they may not know what it is you were trying to communicate. In particular, do not put extraneous evidence in just because that is the way it happened. You can never relate everything. Select those things that support your thesis - the point you are making.

This doesn't mean that I am recommending that you deliberately distort an event or situation to present a one-sided picture. Of course not. Later we will look at deciding the real purpose behind each article. We will assume now that you wish to write an article in a simple even-handed way - just to tell someone something.

GATHERING THE BUILDING BLOCKS

Sometimes, when you are interested in a broad topic, you gather a lot of evidence first. Only after looking at all the research or information that you have accummulated, can you identify the point you wish to make.

Sometimes, in following up an idea, the statement you want to make, the thesis, comes first. Then you seek information, evidence, examples, anecdotes and quotes to support it. These are the building blocks of your article. It is your job to put those building blocks together in such a way that the article does what you want it to do so attractively that it will appeal to many readers.

ARRANGE THE BUILDING BLOCKS

There are as many ways of composing a winning argument as there are debaters to argue. In just the same way, there are many ways of putting together an article which will appeal to first an editor, then to readers. There is no one right way, but all the right ways to write an article are easy for the reader to follow. The information, anecdotes, supporting evidence, etc., are all arranged in such a way that the reader has no difficulty in following your argument from beginning to end.

FIVE COMMON STRUCTURES THAT WORK

As you work through the rest of this chapter you will understand exactly why these structures work. Follow one of these 'patterns' for your first few articles and you will probably sell them.

Once you feel confident in handling your material, then you will develop an intuition as to the best way to present different material and different subjects to different markets. This chapter will get you to that stage.

1 The basic structure

Adaptations of this structure can be used for almost any length, style and type of article.

(a) *The title*
This should be bright, attractive, interesting, exciting or intriguing. It must attract the reader. It is the rosette of ribbon on the package. Since it is best if it says something specific and attention-getting about your subject, perhaps the single diamond ornament in the jeweller's window would be a better analogy.

The title must be relevant. It should give an honest preview of what follows. Don't emulate afternoon newspaper headlines which tempt passers-by into buying by suggesting treasures within their pages which often are not there.

It should use the same style and tone of language as your article, and match the style and tone of your target magazine. Also be aware of the particular circumstances of your readers. Don't, for example, give a title such as 'The Great Crash' to an article you wish to sell to an in-flight magazine: economist J. K. Galbraith was astonished when his best-selling book of that title was not available at airport bookstalls.

The title should be short, crisp, and match the mood of the article. Some specialist magazines and literary and scientific journals prefer long descriptive titles. Always defer to the preferences of the editor to whom you are trying to sell. A snappy title, followed by an explanatory sub-title often is more attractive, and satisfies the needs of academic editors.

If the subject is bizarre, or even unusual, then a title that simply states the subject will be effective.

Use a playful title, such as a play on words, alliteration, paradox, a humorous or provocative statement or question, a quotation or a proverb with a twist in the tail - something that will spark curiosity about what is to follow, for example, 'Through a Glass Starkly', or 'Doing the Bright Thing', etc. Be aware that a pun on a literary or biblical quotation might not be clear to some of your readers, so unless the original is very well-known your version should be able to stand alone, even if the reference is not recognised.

A suitable title often emerges while the article is being written. I find it helpful to have a descriptive working title for the article right from the moment I begin gathering ideas. It helps me focus my thoughts. Then, as I work through the article, I keep my 'antennae' out for a striking title.

It is often a good idea, if a title is not immediately obvious, to brainstorm suggestions when you have finished your first draft. Combine groups of evocative words and phrases until you find the title that works.

Realise, no matter how much you have agonised over finding the perfect title, that it is sometimes changed by the editor, often without consulting you. Be philosophical about this. It is the editor's job to know what will appeal to readers. Or there could be another article scheduled for the same issue, even on the facing page, which uses the same words in its title as the words you chose for yours. When a magazine accepts your article you know that your title was successful; it attracted your first and most important reader - the magazine's editor.

Use normal punctuation within your title, but note that as titles are usually fragments of sentences, they do not have a full-stop at the end. A colon follows a title to link it with a sub-title, if it follows on the same line; if the sub-title is on a different line, then leave the title open-ended (without final punctuation). Sub-titles are punctuated normally.

It is usual to type titles all in capitals, and to type sub-titles in upper and lower case (that is, use upper case only for the first letter of beginning words and any proper nouns).

Sub-titles are not necessary, and are not used in the majority of articles. They certainly should not be considered if your title is factual and self-explanatory. But if your title is a catchy phrase which only becomes clear to the reader with an explanation in the body of the article, then an explanatory sub-title often acts as an additional bait: telling the reader right at the outset what the article is about.

(b) *The eye-catcher or lead*
(also called the Head, Grab-you, Bait, Hook, or Hey!)

This is the first paragraph (or paragraphs, depending on the length of the story) which immediately follows the title, and it is the most important paragraph in your article. In that paragraph *you must make the reader care. You must draw readers into the flow of the article, so that they know they are going somewhere, and they are happy to let you take them there.*

Its first purpose is to invite the readers to stop riffling the pages, and to read your article. Once the readers have paused, you have their attention for the next few seconds or sentences.

Your opening should make them care; it should promise useful, interesting, intriguing or amusing information - in fact, an enjoyable read!

The first paragraph will be all many readers will read, unless a person, an action, or a problem, immediately excites their curiosty. It is your responsibility to create the reaction you want before it is too late, to persuade the readers that an exciting experience is in the offing.

The second purpose is to set out the direction the article is going to take. It draws readers into the flow of the article, so they know where they are going and indicates by the focus and the tone (whether it be didactic, breezy or gently humorous) what kind of journey it will be. Even experienced writers spend a great deal of thought on creating as tempting a lead-paragraph as they can.

Thirdly, the eye-catcher must be an integral part of the story that follows, matching it in every particular - in mood, pace, language, level of difficulty, of erudition, or trendiness. The words with which you introduce your work to readers are the most important words in your article. They must be powerful enough to catch the readers' attention, excite their interest, and entice them to give up some of their time. Yet the readers must never feel that the lead did not keep its promise.

Eye-catchers come in many varieties; choose whatever feels right for the article, keeping an eye on the kind of lead paragraph your target editor (at present that means the editor of the magazine you have chosen for your exercise for Chapter 2) seems most often to prefer.

After catching the readers' attention, lead them into the subject. Tell them what the article is going to be about, and tell them honestly. You may use humour, but do not resort to trickery, nor promise what you cannot deliver. That said, you have a broad choice:

- A narrative opening which leads straight into the body of the article is often effective, particularly if the title or an illustration acts as the eye-catcher, and the subject itself is of unusual interest. This is probably the easiest of all leads to write, and cannot be bettered if the article consists of a tale to be told.

Always be sure you begin where the real story begins. If the article is about sisters, separated as babies by war, who found one another after forty-six years, the real beginning of the story might be where one woman realises her sister is still alive and sets out to find her. The real storyline is in following the set-backs and disappointments that she encounters in her search. The information relating to their separation and the adventures of their lives could be fed in as you tell the real story of one woman's search for her sister. The story would probably climax when they are re-united.

The eye-catcher, then, would be an intriguing paragraph about one sister's discovery, after years of thinking she had no living family, that her sister was still alive. If the discovery was made in dramatic circumstances, so much the better. Make it as enticing as possible, and you and the readers will be away together on a fascinating voyage which can be told in chronological sequence, except for the additional information which will need to be fed in.

- Focusing on one vital detail of your story. This means narrowing your angle down to one attention-grabbing point. From there you open up the subject, explain etc. In your story of the separate sisters, their eventual meeting could be written as a dramatic scene. Then you could go back to the beginning of the search.

- The eye-catcher could be an interesting or powerful quotation from a recognised authority on the subject, or from a famous person whose name alone guarantees attention. Or use a surprising, pithy or humorous quote from someone the reader will meet in the article. A variation which sometimes works is a dialogue between two characters in the article.

- A startling statement, or a sensible statement written in a manner that will intrigue readers, will entice them to read more. Try to think of a sentence in which you encapsulate the core of your thesis. One eye-catcher I will not forget was written by one of my students: 'My mother died for me one day just before lunch. We sat together opposite the specialist, but only I heard the verdict: "Increasingly child-like, irreversible, no treatment." My mother sat happily smiling, smoothing her clothes.' This was the way the student began her story about the slow deterioration and death of her mother from Alzheimer's disease.

- An unusual setting, or even a commonplace setting, can be described in an unusual way. This gives readers an immediate sense of place and time and mood. This is particularly good if the setting is exotic or intriguing. It works well, too, if the main character's personality, behaviour or work, is dependent in some way on the setting.

- Taking the reader into your confidence, as if you are going to relate a fantastic story: 'Imagine for a moment . . .' Just make sure that the story *is* fascinating, so the reader will not feel cheated.

- An anecdote (a small humorous or horrendous story) can illustrate the point you are going to make. The best anecdotes come from your own research, or your own experience, especially if they have the warmth of human interest.

- A cliché or proverb with a twist, or a pun on a well-known saying.

- A direct address or a direct question is the hardest opener of all, but sometimes works well if it leads directly to the next paragraph and into the story. Readers may say, 'Who cares?' Be careful here not to sound preachy or superior. Don't antagonise your readers, woo them.

- An odd or interesting fact that you have uncovered in researching your material.
- A general statement or observation, but once again avoid sounding as if you know it all.
- An accumulation of details builds up interest simply because so many facts are being revealed.
- An unexpected comparison or contrast works well. If you are writing an article about the spoilt socialite daughter of the city's wealthiest man, the information that her best friend is an invalid pensioner living in a very untrendy area of the city is unusual enough to be interesting.
- Introducing yourself, followed by an explanation of why you are writing the article. This approach suggests freshness and honesty if you are leading into a first-person anecdotal article.
- Exaggeration for effect, but be careful here not to make promises you cannot keep.
- Drawing attention to the words themselves, by using alliteration, or quaint, foreign or archaic terminology. This has to be done with discretion and a full awareness of your market.
- Sometimes the eye-catcher is set in larger type, italics or capitals. That is the magazine designer's way of drawing attention to your first paragraph.

Use your own individual way, remembering to connect with your readers. If you care enough to entertain them, enthrall them, intrigue them, and involve their emotions, they will care.

Be aware. Some subjects and some attitudes might touch a sensitive nerve for some readers, so be especially aware that nothing in your tone or words should suggest anything that might be offensive in the slightest degree. This would include showing prejudice of any kind or using a patronising tone. Readers will accept a writer's right to hold and express a personal attitude when this is introduced later in the article, but in the eye-catcher, before you have established rapport, it might be an instant turn-off.

Keep in mind the basic interests of all humankind: food and drink, money, shelter, love, self-improvement, sex.

Never be in a hurry to write the eye-catcher. Even though in the final version it appears at the beginning of your article, it is not a good idea to delay writing the rest of your article until you get the eye-catcher right.

Throughout your preliminary thinking time keep an eye open for a possible eye-catcher. If one is not obvious just sketch out an idea of how you might begin it, and continue with the article. Then develop the sketched idea. You might write and rewrite it three or four, or a dozen, times, before you feel you have it exactly right.

It is essential that it is the best you can do, for if it is weak, your most important reader, the editor, may never accept your invitation to read the body of your article.

Avoid being wordy or trite, pretentious or preachy. Reach out to your readers and invite them to come with you.

(c) *Your thesis*

This is a clear statement of the point you want to make. This may be directly stated or implied, but it must be unmistakeable.

Your thesis carries the message that you want readers to remember long after they have forgotten the rest of the article. A strong, clear message is most memorable and most saleable.

(d) *Reader involvement*

Why should the readers care? If your thesis is relevant to all humanity your reader will care. If it is not, then you can explicitly or implicitly point out why this thesis is important to that particular reader. People have differing needs - to be informed, to be reassured, to be entertained – so your thesis need not be world-shattering to be effective.

(e) *Your credentials*

You have another opportunity here to connect with readers. You have a chance to tell them something specific about yourself, something that will make you stand out as a particular communicator, something that will encourage each reader to like you, identify with you.

The body, which comprises the main part of the article, will prove to readers whether or not you know what you are talking about. This is another advantage the non-fiction writer has over the fiction writer. You can introduce yourself, cite your authority, establish your credibility, tell the readers why they should listen to, and believe you. This, too, can be spelt out or implied.

Your credentials may be implicit because of your article's position in the magazine. If you contribute as an authority in the health, gardening or cookery section the editor's judgement of your credentials will be respected.

Otherwise, tell the readers why they should believe you:

I was there.

It happened to me, or my mother . . .

I spent three months researching it.

I interviewed 30 000 prisoners, and this is what they told me.

I picked the child up out of the gutter.

My academic qualifications give me authority.

Sometimes credentials are explicitly stated in the sub-title or the eye-catcher. Sometimes credentials are divorced from the main text and boxed in a side-bar. Sometimes your credentials are given at the end of the article.

The most important reason for establishing your credentials is to encourage readers to like and trust you, so they will read on. The easiest and best way to encourage readers to like you is to like your readers, and to let them see that you do by the tone of your writing.

(f) *The body of the article*

This is where you say what you have to say. This part comprises at least three-quarters of the article. Within the framework that precedes it (the title, the eye-catcher, the thesis, and perhaps reader involvement and your credentials) and that which follows it (the summary and closure), the body of the article has its own structure. There are several formal structures which work very well, and innumerable others that work in special cases.

All writers develop a sensibility that enables them intuitively to craft an article that fits together like a seamless garment - an individual shape that is perfect for that article and no other. If you don't feel confident enough to trust this ability yet, then follow one of the following frameworks. They have been used successfully countless times. They work. Build your article by following one of these blueprints and you will create a well-balanced, coherent and saleable story.

Here are some of the easiest, most adaptable and most effective ways of developing a convincing argument. They all have several features in common. Every article 'body' has a logical shape within which you have to make your points, and unless they are self-evident you will have to supply supporting evidence in the form of acceptable quotations, statistics (provable), anecdotes, examples, etc.

- The three-point shape.

  This, of course, is not limited to three points. You could make more, but less than three is usually not convincing. There is something magical about the number three. A reader given three 'proofs' will usually believe.

Using this system, the most basic and adaptable of all, just think about your thesis and think of three strong points which you want to make about it. These points are the framework behind the thesis. They will convince the reader that your thesis is justifiable, good sense, understandable, and so on.

If possible, each of these points should have three pieces of supporting material (such as anecdotes, examples, quotations, statistics, etc.) which either strengthen or illustrate the point. A suitable anecdote could illustrate the point. A quotation could be from classical sources, or from yesterday's interview, as long as it adds depth to the illustrative material.

The argument is more effective if the three major points are arranged in order of increasing weight or intensity. This allows you to build up towards your key idea, thus creating tension. This applies also to each supporting point, putting the weakest example first, and the most telling last. This builds up suspense about the outcome. However, it works best if early in the story you have hinted at the strength, horror, sadness, and so on, of the outcome. Advice for playwrights is that if a gun is shown hanging on the wall in the first act, it must be fired before the final curtain falls. That is valid for non-fiction, too. But so is the obverse. If the gun is going to fire a fatal shot before the end of the story or play, it must be shown or hinted at early in the story. This allows reader-involvement.

- Time shape: past, present, future.
  If you want to write about traffic congestion on the Sydney Harbour Bridge, you might divide the body of your article into three sections: first, outline the past history of the bridge and how for its first forty years its capacity was adequate; then detail aspects of present traffic conditions on the bridge; last, state what is planned for its future. Each period would need to be supported by statistics, illustrations, descriptions, etc.

- Any series of three gradations.
  Examples are youth, middle-life, age; small, medium, large; cheap, medium-priced, expensive - of hospital care, holidays, pantyhose, or anything else. If it seems more effective, the order could be reversed.

- List shape.
  An example could be 'Ten ways to make a million dollars'. These may also need explanations to support them. In this case it is usually better to begin and end with strong points. If you have weak points, put them somewhere in the middle, and make sure the supporting points are either entertaining or strongly convincing.

- Problem and solution.
  The simplest examples are recipes, or other instructions. This broad format can also be used for how-to articles, and expanded for any other problem you want to present to readers and then follow with a solution. All, except for the simplest recipe example, will need to have supporting material if they are to be convincing.

- Comparison or contrast.
  Use the similarities of like things, or the dissimilarities of unlike things, to make your point. Use strongly relevant anecdotes and examples.

- Arguments for and against.
  This is usually done by detailing not only why, but who is for it and who is against it. Stronger, too, if you conclude by recommending - with convincing reasons - why one course of action should be followed.

- Short and long-range views of the subject.

- The big picture.
  This would then narrow down to a specific important single case, or the reverse.

As you can see, any logical shape can be used, as long as it is logical, not just a random scattering of ideas and information.

(g) *The summary*

Repeat briefly what you have already told your readers. Be clear. Readers should not have to guess your message. Apart from summarising, you can also speculate on how the events will affect the readers or the world; that is, take the argument one step further. In the summary writers bring the readers in a full circle, back to where they began. (I think a spiral may be an even better analogy.) At this point you and your readers should be closer to understanding or enlightenment than when you started.

(h) *The close*

Sometimes this is not necessary, but after summing up a final thought is often needed. In an article aimed at persuasion, you might need to tell the reader what to do. Sometimes an apt thought, or quote, provides a suitable last sentence.

Sometimes an anecdote begun in the eye-catcher can be completed at the close. This is effective, but must be logical.

Whatever you choose, whether you end with the summary or add an additional paragraph, don't let it just die away. The article must end with a decided *thump!* You may be able to induce a chuckle or a sob, but it must be obvious that you have reached the end. You must leave your reader satisfied. If your first line says, 'Come, join me! Travel with me for a while', a reader must say on reading your last line, 'I'm glad I came. It was a good trip.'

All other successful article structures have much in common with this basic structure. They all need a succinct title; they all need an eye-catching first paragraph, they all need to progress logically and coherently towards a pre-planned ending which should be satisfying for the readers. You will learn to fashion many kinds of structure to suit your material. A brief outline of a few other popular structures follows.

2 My BEST method

This is really a simplification of the basic structure. It is useful for short articles; it is a good check to make sure that all the information follows in a logical sequence, and that nothing has been forgotten. It is particularly useful for anecdotal articles and personal essays and stories told chronologically. The comments about the components in the more detailed basic structure all apply.

- **B** stands for *bait.*
  You must entice your readers to 'bite' by the combination of title and eye-catching paragraph. The bait hooks the readers.

- **E** stands for *explanation.*
  Tell your readers what you are going to write about, state your thesis, or put your proposal.

- **S** stands for the first *step,* supported by the first piece of evidence, or in many cases, the first anecdote.
  This is followed by the second and third steps, and as many further steps as you like, as long as they all lead steadily in the same direction. Keep your readers on the track until you reach your conclusion. Don't lead them off into by-ways and side-tracks. With personal essays the tone of the writing is all-important and the writer usually has more leeway. But keep it interesting. Filmmaker Alfred Hitchcock said that 'Drama is life with the dull bits cut out.' The same applies to a successful article. The best essayists manage to hold their readers' interest by introducing gentle drama even to the most mundane topics.

- **T** stands for *termination* (the end, the concluding summary). It could be the thesis restated or it could be the answer, the proof, the outcome, or perhaps just a clearer picture of the world, that you are showing your readers.

3 The inverted pyramid

You will be familiar with this article structure from reading newspaper stories and press releases. They have all their most important facts crammed up at the top. The first paragraph tells us who, what, where, when and how. There is no tension, no careful balancing of incidents, no effort to win over the readers.

The subsequent paragraphs contain subsidiary or supporting information arranged in order of decreasing importance.

I understand that the reason for this shape is to allow a sub-editor to cut off the end of the story if space becomes tight, without losing the main point. I cannot think of anything else in favour of this shape.

4 The *Washington Post* style

This type of article begins with a particular instance, usually a graphic example, a vivid action scene, then the broader issues surrounding the subject are discussed. The dramatic scene of the sisters meeting to open the story of the separation would be one example of this. This is similar to a bull's-eye shape, which can be used for the body of the basic structure. The central issue is described first, then peripheral matters, which sometimes explain it, are discussed. The action is placed in context; the history and surrounding circumstances are explained. The reason or thesis of the story is made clear.

It has the advantage of immediately grabbing readers' attention.

5 Exhaustive research

I hesitate to call this a 'method'. First, collect all possible information on a subject, mull over ideas, read reference books, seek out as many interviews as possible, and bring together everything you can think of related to the topic. Then sort all the information into a cohesive shape and discard what doesn't fit.

This is extremely time-consuming, but for some stories (such as historical and biographical articles) it often seems to be the only way of doing it. There is usually a lot of material you cannot use, but you may be able to write other articles for different markets using some of the discarded information.

This method, with its enormous breadth of research, is more suitable for non-fiction books. For articles it is far less time-consuming, and it is less daunting, to know what information you need, before you start detailed researching.

SIDE-BARS

These are separate blocks of type (often in boxes) which appear beside or in the middle of articles. They are usually differentiated (by different type, or by shading, double-spacing, being enclosed in a heavy border, or by a combination of these) to make them stand out.

- Side-bars are used to include relevant material which would interrupt the writing flow if included in the main part of your article.

- Side-bars change the pace. In a heavily scientific or technical article a human interest story which depicts your subject would add interest, and the readers may very well read the story in the side-bar, and then decide to read the technical evidence. Or the reverse. Hard, authoritative data that supports the thesis, which you have written about in an anecdotal manner, and which, if included in the main story, would change the mood and interrupt the flow, would be better in a side-bar.

- They can induce reader-involvement. A test or quiz (with answers) could be included so that the readers could test themselves on the theme of your article. If you are recommending exercise for health for people over eighty, you could run a quiz to assess readers' health based on their answers to questions. For this example you would need medical advice, but some quizzes are purely for fun and then you can be as outrageous as you like.

- Side-bars include basic information, such as 'How to get there' for travel articles, or 'Where to buy it'.

- They are useful for presenting lists (of, say, the ten best available touring bicycles to go with an article on 'Touring the Hunter Valley Wineries by Bicycle').

- Side-bars make a long and/or complex article easier to organise.

Editors and designers like using side-bars to break up the solid blocks of type of an unillustrated article. The material is usually paid for at the same word-count rate as the main article.

When submitting the article, write the side-bar on a separate page headed 'Side-bar for Title of Article', then under that give the side-bar its own title, and mention it in your covering letter.

Exercises

1 Analyse your chosen article. You probably will not want to use it strictly as a model. But this is the article that particular editor chose to print. It is written in the style thought appropriate for the magazine's readers. So examine it thoroughly, analyse it carefully and make notes on:

(a) Title - long or short?

(b) How does the writer draw attention to this article? Why did you stop turning pages to read it?

(c) Isolate the eye-catcher - why did it catch your eye?

(d) Can you work out the structure of the article? Good writing is seamless. The 'bones' shouldn't be obvious, but now you know what to look for, perhaps you can work out what structure 'your' editor prefers.

(e) Pay particular attention to the means used to convince you. Did the writer use anecdotes, statistics, or other 'proofs'?

(f) How did the writer bring the article to a convincing end?

2 Pin the answers to these question onto the chosen article and put it in the folder with the notes for your first article.

3 If you have time, and particularly if on closer examination you begin to feel that this article will not serve as a suitable model, go through the other ten selected articles, and make a second choice. Then analyse that one in similar depth.

4

KNOW YOUR PURPOSE AND YOUR AUDIENCE

WHY ARE YOU WRITING THIS ARTICLE?

What is the purpose of your article? What do you plan to achieve?

There are five main purposes for all communication: all writing, all conversation, all oration (talks, lectures, etc.), are either to inform, persuade, make an observation (to share your view of the world), make a judgement or an evaluation, or to evoke an emotion.

Think about the primary role you will be playing as the writer of your projected article. Is it to be as reporter, persuader, observer, evaluater, or as one who inspires or evokes emotion? Also there will almost always be an element of entertainment. In most articles these roles will overlap, but the best writers carefully select the appropriate voice, language, style and subject matter to achieve most effectively their desired objectives with their readers.

What do you wish to do?

- To inform or report? Is there some subject or aspect of a subject which you wish to explain, instruct, teach, demonstrate, or clarify? This is a factual article, and it can be almost totally objective; it can also be thoughtful and insightful. Accuracy is essential, and research is often necessary. Historical articles, scientific, educational and news reports are the kind used by writers to inform their readers.

While the title or eye-catcher may grab the readers' initial attention, the best way to ensure that they keep reading until you have imparted your information is to connect your new information with something the readers already know. Go from the known, the easily recognisable, to the unknown. Nearly two thousand years ago Jesus used this method to teach. In the parables He did not speak of theology or philosophy, He spoke of grapes and fish - those things with which His listeners were very familiar.

In an informative article it is better to use a sharing-of-knowledge tone rather than that of a lecture.

- To persuade? If you wish to influence, convince, motivate, preach, change an attitude or stimulate someone to action, you will write an article of persuasion. In a travel article the purpose is usually to persuade readers to visit a particular place.

  The wonderful sights and exotic customs you describe, and the information about the bargain prices you report, are what will lead readers to succumb to your persuasion. It is in an article of persuasion that you most often call upon the readers to act - to go on that holiday!

  When writing an article with which you hope to persuade readers to some course of action, you will measure everything you write against the effect it will have on your readers.

- To observe? If you wish to tell of your responses to the world and its people, focus on yourself and your relationship with your world. To be a sensitive observer you must be attuned to the internal and external environment. You will be at your best in a biographical essay.

  This type of article includes diaries, personal essays, inspirational and art-of-living articles. The writer's personality and emotions play a big part in these articles. Writers as observers write more subjectively than in other roles. The style is often discursive, and the tone may be that of a personal discussion or of a light-hearted tale.

- To evaluate? This is when you give your educated and/or authoritative opinion - when you review books, theatre, restaurants, world affairs, etc. You will observe and carefully weigh the evidence, and will almost certainly have a better-than-average knowledge of the subject you are evaluating.

  Readers will need to be convinced that, even though you may be biased, such bias will be freely admitted, so that your article will give the impression that all sides have been considered and your summing-up will be seen as an educated assessment.

- To evoke emotion? Do you wish to inspire, amuse, entertain, celebrate, induce anger, reduce to laughter, or evoke sympathy? The prime purpose of a plea for sympathy, a comedy sketch, a dictator's rhetoric and a fanatic's tirade is to evoke an emotion (of one kind or another) in their readers.

Most communication, most stories, have multiple purposes, but one is usually dominant. Think about the article you plan to write. Are you quite clear why you are writing it? Are you quite sure what your objective is?

You will write more easily when you write with a purpose, and more effectively when you are fully aware of that purpose. When you know what you want to say, and you know why you want to say it, you will write with power and passion. You will write to make a difference.

When you care, you are more likely to keep your readers' attention, despite the competing demands on their time of other reading matter, television, radio, and numerous other activities.

WHO IS YOUR READER?

Who are you writing for? What is your target market?

Your audience will be drawn from the population of the world, but that is too general even for the most popular and successful writers. You must define that segment of the world's, or more realistically the country's, population towards which you will aim your article.

In order to know what they would like to read, you need to know them. Do you know your readers' age, sex, education level, language facility, marital status, income, attitude to luxury (covetousness or disdain), political leanings, religious affiliations, if any, place of residence (country or city), profession or job (white-collar, blue-collar, unemployed, student, self-employed, retired), attitude to a whole range of things (such as the environment, migration, overseas investment, abortion, etc.)?

You will never know all the answers, but you should know enough to make an educated guess.

You can't write for people you don't know

If you are a struggling student from a working-class home, you will find it difficult to write for magazines catering for the wealthy - those people who have everything. On the other hand, if you have never been hungry, if you have never been torn by the conflict of whether to buy new school shoes for your little daughter or to pay the grocery bill, then it is unlikely that you can write for people who are struggling to make ends meet - unless you are prepared to do some on-the-spot research.

Australian novelist Kylie Tennant was such a thorough researcher that before she wrote her novels she lived in the social milieu of her characters. She was so anxious to get the tone as well as the details exactly right that she lived in a slum, and even went to gaol. For *The Honey Flow,* a novel about itinerant bee-keepers, she went on the road as a migratory honey-collector. It is unlikely that you will be able to afford the time for such intensive involvement for an article.

To the adage that *you can only write about what you know* you must add the corollary that *you write best for people you know.* You will connect more easily and thus more believably with readers whose base knowledge or experience you at least appreciate, even if you don't share it. If you try to write about a life-style, experience, or city with which you are not familiar, you will make mistakes - and someone will notice those mistakes. They always do, and frequently write to the editor of the magazine, pointing them out with glee. Recently I noticed in an American magazine a reference to the film-character Crocodile Dundee as an Australian 'bush-ranger'!

Your attitude

You are a professional, even if only part-time. 'Amateurs talk about writing. Professionals talk about markets' - this has been said a thousand times, and remains as true as ever. You won't be rewarded because you wrote the article. You will be rewarded only if someone wants to *buy* it. Therefore, keep your audience in mind - their desires, and the things that matter to them. Readers need to get something for themselves out of every story they read.

What are your readers' pre-conceptions about your topic? How have you dealt with them?

The requirements of a particular market

Think about your market. Where will you sell your article?

Browse through every magazine, every newspaper - every

possible market - that comes to your notice. Study them from cover to cover.

Keep buying regularly the publications you like best, for they are the ones you will find easiest to sell to. If you like reading the magazine, the other readers are likely to have much in common with you. Writing for your readers, then, will be not too different from writing for yourself.

Don't only read the articles, also read the fiction, the letters to the editor, the editorial, and, most particularly, the advertisements. If it seems to be a likely market, write to the editor of the magazine and ask for an information sheet outlining guidelines for contributors and the philosophy of the magazine. This alone will not be enough. The editor will also expect that you can assess who the magazine's readers are by reading the magazine.

Through the editor's eyes

Each magazine aims precisely at its readers. The editorial and staff-written pieces will help you see exactly *who* the editor has in mind. You have to get to know those readers.

In the editorial the editor will reveal the interests, sometimes the sex and the education level, of readers by the subject matter, the tone and the language used.

See if you can identify the staff-written pieces. Staff-writers and contributing editors will be aiming precisely at the target readers. Study their work.

Through the readers' eyes

Special sections for readers' contributions and letters to the editor identify even more clearly who the readers are.

Use the advertisers' market research

As a result of their market research advertising agencies focus precisely on the markets for their products. If the advertisements are for expensive cars, imported leather luggage, diamond cuff-links and bracelets, then you can be sure that the readers of that magazine will include people with an income high enough to buy those items. It would probably not be a likely market for your article on how to back-pack to the Glasshouse Mountains, sleeping in youth hostels on the way.

Advertisements are important in another way, too. They provide a large proportion of the income for most magazines. The money to pay for your article comes from the advertisements, so it is unlikely that an editor would publish anything (including your brilliant article) that would antagonise the magazine's advertisers.

I learned this the hard way very early in my writing life. I wrote a light-hearted article which was highly critical of television advertising and the detrimental effect many advertisements have on children. It was returned with a charming letter from the editor in which she said she agreed with my opinions, but pointed out that her magazine depended upon the advertisements from the very firms I was criticising.

How much do readers know?

If you are writing for a scientific journal in which the editorial and other material is of a highly technical nature, then go ahead and use your most technical terms. You are writing for an in-group.

However, if you are writing for a general-interest magazine about the same scientific subject, take care to use the common terms, and to explain anything which might puzzle a scientifically uneducated person, and relate the outcomes to everyday things.

When you write for such an audience be very careful not to talk down to them. They are probably cleverer at any number of things than you are. What you have to be clear about is what knowledge and general understanding you share. It is shared prior knowledge and shared vocabulary that makes communication possible.

Select your market

1 As soon as you choose an idea, decide on a group of markets. List six magazines which might buy it.

2 Study your target magazines for length, viewpoint, reader-reaction, titles, etc.

3 Try to find a perfect match – the market where your article will fit exactly. If you find more than one, then choose first the best-paying market or the editor who pays on acceptance.

4 Try to focus exactly on one reader, one editor, one magazine, one reading group. It is essential to choose the correct slant for the particular reader.

A few years ago, after querying and getting the go-ahead from a magazine aimed at upwardly mobile career-women, I wrote an article about an intensive course for executive secretaries and the success stories of several of its graduates. After doing the course, they had entered the executive stream of their own or other companies, started their own businesses, etc. This magazine decided not to publish my article because it focused on the success of several women; they preferred articles which focused on just one successful woman.

I then offered it to an in-flight magazine. The editor there passed it on to a colleague, the editor of a sister-magazine whose editor identified his readers as upwardly mobile tertiary-educated young male executives about thirty-five years old. This editor liked the article, but asked that I rewrite it; change the viewpoint from that of the participating executive secretary to that of her boss, the male executive. In other words, the *boss* should read the article and learn about the course for his secretary.

I rewrote the story as he asked.

Interesting feed-back came when I later spoke to many of the secretaries who attended subsequent courses: every one of them had read the article in the journal which was supposedly aimed at the male executives. The secretaries had then told their bosses about the course, and had asked to participate in it.

Even editors are not always exact in their targeting.

Keep up-to-date

Television and the advertising industry has changed our way of perceiving and accepting information. A TV-conditioned person absorbs rapid visual images from all over the world. Advertising is the most extreme example of this rapid-fire information exchange.

You may not *like* the way TV advertising, indeed many of the modern ways of communicating, have changed our world, but you must *know* what the advertisements are doing - you must recognise what they are doing to the audience, to your audience, to all of us.

Print media remains the choice of many simply because readers have the freedom to make their own selection, proceeding at their own pace. But never lose sight of the fact that everyone today has been influenced by the communication revolution. It is unlikely that Charles Dickens, Anthony Trollope, George Eliot, or even Jane Austen, would be published if they submitted their novels to a publisher today. Their writing was right for readers of the nineteenth century; brilliant as their work is, today's average reader, accustomed to a faster pace of life, television and films, often finds them slow going.

Exercises

Write five very short articles (150–250 words), each with a different major purpose; for example:

1 Report an interesting event or occasion for your local paper, or for a magazine you read regularly.

2 Write a short travel piece designed to coax holidaymakers to a place you recently visited, even if it is only your local park.

3 Share your view of the world with well-defined readers (perhaps a comment on a family situation), something about which the readers will say, 'That's life!' or 'That's the way people are!'

4 Review a book, a play, a lecture, or a restaurant (preferably a recent experience), one that you have not seen reviewed.

5 Write an inspirational or humorous piece for a market which you can clearly identify.

These may not be marketable – not yet, anyway. But if you have carefully examined your role as you write each article, and have kept the reading audience in mind, you will have learned much about what you write best, and what you enjoy writing.

5

LANGUAGE

Never underestimate the power of language. Language not only expresses our thoughts, it influences our thoughts and our behaviour. I know a woman who is afraid of cancer, so afraid that she cannot bring herself to say the word 'cancer'! She goes to her doctor to check on some pain, and she says something like, 'You don't think it's . . . you know, doctor, that terrible thing?' I am told that, in their locker-rooms, some otherwise tough, confident men refer to cancer as 'the big C'. Do they really think that by their avoidance of the word 'cancer' they are protecting themselves from the reality of cancer? It seems so.

In St John's Gospel the power of language is made clear: 'In the beginning was the word, and the word was with God, and the word was God.' From the beginning of civilisation the lives of men and women have been directed by, and experienced through, spoken and written words.

Language is the prime tool of writers. I shall assume, because you are using this book, that you have a real interest in language as a tool for communicating.

All communication, be it writing or speaking or mime, transfers an idea from one mind to another. In writing, particularly, the clarity and accuracy with which the idea is transferred depends upon the clear, accurate and unambiguous use of words. For words to be completely effective the reader must have exactly the same understanding of the meaning of each word as the writer. It would never do if, like

Humpty Dumpty in *Alice Through the Looking Glass,* we said, 'When I use a word, it means just what I want it to mean - neither more nor less.'

In writing, much more than in any face-to-face communication, the words, these black marks on white paper, are the only tools a writer has to communicate with; the better we understand how to use these tools, the better we communicate. The words, though they have a power of their own are, first of all, only a tool to express thoughts. The *thought* is what you are trying to communicate. The thought is more important than the words.

Some writers write with an easy-to-follow smoothness, no matter what they are writing about. Even when the subject is complicated or new, we don't need to struggle to be interested, to follow, to understand. Perhaps such writers were born with this gift, perhaps they painstakingly learned and practised how to use words in this magical way. However they came by their present skill, the only tools they use are words, the same words that are available to you and to me.

Good writing is usually expressed as readability or style.

Readability and style are equally important. If you consciously try to make your writing as readable as you can, consciously clear the path for your readers and lead them along that path, allowing them to experience the story you are unfolding as a discovery of their own, then you will do it in your own particular style. Style is how you use words. It is much more an unconscious expression of the person you are, after you have consciously worked on making your story readable.

Though you, the writer, do most of the work, readers do not remain passive. If they continue to read, readers evaluate, assess, and agree or disagree with your thesis. Your readers either accept your ideas or discard them.

If your readers know nothing of you or your subject, you have to win their interest, their trust. You have to hold the readers with such genuine thoughtfulness that by the time they finish reading the article they not only trust you but also respect and like you.

You have to be aware of how much you have to explain; you have to know when you need to repeat for emphasis or clarity. You have to know when enough is enough, when more will bore. That takes readability and style.

READABILITY

Your aim as a writer is to communicate, so your first concern must always be to keep the readers reading. As we have seen in Chapter 3, readability also depends much upon logical structure. But how we use words also makes the difference between an article that sings and one that plods. Remember, thoughts have to be clear, as well as the words. It is the thoughts which must be presented with clarity.

Thoughts cannot be presented with clarity, however, unless they have breathing space. Each thought should be presented separately - one thought per sentence. Don't overload your sentences. Heavily loaded sentences make for laboured reading.

You don't want your readers to have to read and reread each sentence. They may give up, exhausted. Each sentence should lead smoothly, without gaps, to the next sentence. That calls for intelligent use of transitions.

Each sentence should be staged according to its importance within the paragraph. Generally a paragraph deals with one idea only. The last sentence is most often the strongest or weightiest. The first sentence is the next strongest. Arrange your sentences in such a way that the first sentence introduces your thought, then builds up to the most important point in the final sentence of your paragraph. But variety is also important. There is a place for paragraphs of a different construction whose purpose is to change the pace of the story.

Stage your information

Serve it invitingly, don't dish it out in great heaps. This applies particularly where a lot of background information has to be given. Write it in sensitively, being careful not to interrupt the flow of the story. Sometimes a quiet moment can be used; sometimes it is best to feed in the information between action paragraphs. Above all, don't do it in such a way that readers see you, the writer, intruding.

Description

Because messages are interpreted and integrated in the mind, one of the best ways to communicate is to create visual images - to build pictures. While similes and metaphors add colour and spice to your writing, the simplest way to build mental pictures is with description that is concrete and specific.

Sometimes it may be best to start with general information and then to move on to specific details. Or the reverse. Don't lose your readers. Make sure they know what you are describing. If you move to another description, give your readers notice that you are shifting your focus.

Use your judgement; the story comes first. If you are describing a girl running desperately for her life, don't interrupt the action with a description of her clothes, even if they do help to characterise her.

Appeal to all five senses. Open up your decriptions to include what you hear and smell and feel and taste, as well as what you see. An unusual richness will be your reward.

Be as brief as it is possible to be with effectiveness. Readers are likely to be less tolerant of long descriptive passages in non-fiction than in fiction. Use two or three words instead of as many sentences. Short descriptions are best interspersed with whatever action and narrative there is, not lumped together in a long separate paragraph.

Description can be literal, or suggestions which evoke the image without too much detail. A mix of both often works best.

- Readers are more interested in people than in things. Often a place can be depicted and enlivened by describing the people in the place, or of the place. The reverse works well, too. When it is necessary to fully characterise a person, an in-depth description will need to be a mixture of general impressions and details, physical and otherwise. If this is backed up with some observations about the surroundings or background it will deepen your characterisation.

- Be selective. Though you may know a thousand descriptive details about your subject, *use only those details that do the job you want done* - which lead the readers where you want them to go. You might know the life history and the entire family of a neighbour, but if you want to write an article about his travel adventures, then use only those details that build the picture of him as an adventurer/traveller (even though he may also be a rose-grower, a devoted father of seven, a teacher at the local technical college, an avid collector of early Chinese porcelain and an elder of his church).

  You may want to use *one* of these very different aspects of his character to highlight, emphasise or contrast with his adventurous spirit, or to show him as a fuller, more rounded character. But be careful to include in your article only that information which will contribute to the point you want to make. Use only the information that best serves the story you are telling at this time.

- Be wary of typecasting. You may wish to describe a woman sitting alone in a bar having a drink. You can say she is sitting quietly in a corner, sipping her drink, or you can say she is young and pretty, and all the men are looking at her. Both may be true, but if you only choose one part of the description then your readers will see a character built on the typecasting of our society.

Study how successful authors make description a singing part of their prose. Look at Jan Morris's *Journeys* (OUP, 1984) and Walter Murdoch's essays. In 'On Vastness' Murdoch writes that we should not be afraid of the Earth colliding with a comet, for it 'is believed to be of no great size; and the tail is of a marvellous tenuity - it is thinner than a minor poet's verse' (*Selected Essays*, Angus & Robertson, Sydney, 1956, p. 101).

Use concrete nouns

Common nouns (such as *dog, tree, fence*) are stronger than abstract nouns (such as *truth, honour, poverty*). Common nouns are easily seen, instantly visualised. Precise nouns (such as *spaniel, gum-tree, picket-fence*) are even stronger because they evoke a more vivid, a more distinct picture. On the other hand, abstract nouns remain an idea, not a picture. Use abstract nouns with care, for it is more difficult to transfer thoughts which neither you nor your readers can visualise. For example, when you would write of poverty, illustrate the concept by writing of a family unable to afford shelter, who camp in summer under bridges, and in winter send the children to stay with relatives.

Do not use meaningless fudge-words, such as *aspect, element, factor,* and *situation*. These are words used by journalists and commentators too lazy to find the right word. Fashions come and go. Probably before you read this, other empty words will have appeared. You will recognise them because they mean nothing, and they do not contribute anything towards understanding. Avoid them. They deaden your writing.

Be specific

Don't make generalisations; they are fuzzy and prevent clarity. It is better to be specific, to write not of the mass but of something particular. Don't try to describe a herd of cattle, describe one cow. When writing of gifted children, don't try to describe them all but write of how a ten-year-old taught you to use a computer.

If your thought cannot be stated clearly and simply, then your idea is not profound, merely unclear. If you can't explain something so a child can understand it then you don't know enough to write about it.

The more specific details you give, the better the picture you build for your reader. Gabriel Garcia Marquez, a journalist as well as the celebrated author of *One Hundred Years of Solitude, Love in the Time of Cholera* and other novels, felt that such details need not even be realistic or possible to be convincing. 'If you say there are elephants flying in the sky, people are not going to believe you', he said, 'But if you say that there are four hundred and twenty-five elephants in the sky, people will probably believe you' (quoted in George Plimpton (ed.), *The 'Paris Review' Interviews*, sixth series, Secker & Warburg, London, 1985, p. 324).

A more realistic example is 'The boy in the blue shirt'; this is better than merely 'The boy'. It helps to build a quick picture of the boy. Even better is 'The tow-haired boy in the blue shirt munching an apple'. What about 'The bare-foot blond urchin in the blue shirt clutched a scrunched-up paper bag as he stood munching an apple'? This is a vivid picture which everyone can see. But have we lost sight of our purpose? Are we still leading our readers where we want them to go?

Keep on track

Take care to direct your readers. For example, do not paint a vivid picture of the above-mentioned scruffy boy if it leads the readers in the wrong direction. If what you are really trying to do is describe the ocean-going yachts as they come into Hobart's Constitution Dock at the end of the Sydney–Hobart yacht race, and the boy happens to be a fellow-watcher, it may be better not to paint a vivid picture of him, but to save your picture-building for the main point of interest.

In other words, do not tell the readers where *not* to go. Instead, lead the readers carefully from the beginning of your story to the end, making sure that they do not lose their way or follow side-tracks.

Transitions

Lead your readers from one point to another. Transitions are the bridges to make sure readers do not lose their way. We are all familiar with transitions such as 'Meanwhile, back at the ranch . . .'

They need not be clichés, but transitions are necessary to interlock one scene with the next.

- Time-and-place changes are bridged smoothly by such words and phrases as:
  That night as I reached my door . . .
  Next day when she went to her car . . .
  A few days later . . .
  It wasn't until the next spring . . .
  Such time-and-place links usually work best when the transitional phrase or word *begins* a paragraph.

- Ideas also have to be linked by connecting words or phrases to ensure that readers are still following your central thought; this is even more important in longer, complicated articles. Transitional words such as *accordingly, finally, similarly, then,* etc., are worth their space, even in a short article.

- Emotional changes are also more smoothly handled by the use of transitions, for example,
  Something happened, so she thought . . .
  Because of (such and such), I no longer trusted him . . .

These steps from one state of mind to another are better handled *within* a paragraph.

- Repeating a word or phrase also helps to bridge a gap, to remind the readers that this is another step along a well-defined pathway. Sometimes it acts as additional evidence - another proof, another example - to support an idea previously expressed. Sometimes a repeated word or phrase will provide an echo to link a completely different idea to the whole thesis, so then it acts as a familiar word or phrase to hold the whole argument together.

> There is always a sneer in Las Vegas. The mountains around it sneer. The desert sneers. And arrogant in the middle of its wide valley, dominating those diligent sprawling suburbs, the downtown city sneers like anything. (Jan Morris, 'Las Vegas, USA', *Journeys*, p. 24)

- A quote which is itself remarkable, or is spoken by a remarkable person, often serves as an attention-getting introduction or transition to a new subject area. Jan Morris also uses quotes from residents to introduce new areas. Her small dialogue with a hotel maid in Texas is memorable: the author asked the maid where she was from, and the girl answered, 'I'm not from nowhere. I'm from Mexico' (*Journeys*, p. 124).

- A question, which is posed implicitly or explicitly, can be answered within a leap into another subject. The link of answer to the previous question will provide a convincing transition. In Alan Marshall's *In Mine Own Heart* (Cheshire, 1963, p. 192) he describes his camp on the road, where he is joined by a young out-of-work traveller during the Great Depression:

> We sit side by side in this bright cell beyond which was the world we were challenging. Curly's mate was out there

> somewhere. He had a mate. Maybe he was lying by the railway thirty miles back with a bloody stump where his leg had been.
>
> 'I don't think Blue could have tripped', he said . . .

and Marshall goes on to describe in great detail the hazards of jumping on and off moving trains, a mode of travelling forced on many men during the depression.

Examine the effectiveness of the connecting words and phrases carefully. When you read your work through, pretend that it was written by someone whom you don't know, or don't like. Can you follow the story every step along the way without wavering? Would you trust this writer? Are you, as a sceptical reader, convinced, won over?

Correctness

Know your *grammar*. I do not have space here to deal with the tricky business of English grammar. If you feel you didn't get a clear understanding at school, or if you have forgotten many of the rules, there are many elementary grammar books available cheaply. I particularly recommend William Strunk Jr and E. B. White's *The Elements of Style* (3rd edn, Macmillan, New York, 1979). Easily the best way to learn anything is to look it up as you need it. Soon you won't need it.

Verbs

Pay special attention to tricky verbs like 'to lay' and 'to lie'. The present tense of the transitive verb 'to lay' is 'lay', as in 'I lay the parcel down'. The past tense of that sentence would be 'I laid the parcel down'. Oddly, some newspaper journalists frequently misspell this as 'layed'.

The present tense of the intransitive verb 'to lie' is 'lie', as in 'I lie on the bed.' The past tense of that sentence is 'I lay on the bed.'

To complicate this further, if by 'lie' you refer to telling a falsehood, the present tense is 'I lie when I am frightened'. The past tense of that sentence is 'I lied when I was frightened'.

There are many such inconsistencies. For example, pictures are 'hung', but people are 'hanged'.

Those of us who were drilled thoroughly in grammar and usage when we were at school now use the rules without thinking. Those who learnt English later in life as a second or third language, or those who had less strict teachers, may have to brush-up on the rules of grammar and usage.

It *is* important. Someone who reads what you write will notice that you have made a mistake. If it is the editor of your target magazine, then it may mean you won't make the sale.

Pronouns

Correctly link all pronouns. Make it quite clear to which nouns pronouns refer. 'Terry and Margaret visited their cousins' house after lunch. They were surprised to learn they had left the city.' Who had left the city? And who were surprised by it? You don't want your readers to stop reading your article to ask such questions.

Clauses

Beware of dangling clauses. 'After travelling widely throughout the world, Scotland is still my favourite place.' Such a clause can only refer to the subject, Scotland, and Scotland cannot travel.

Punctuation

This provides timing. When speaking, you would pause. When writing, allow a comma, a semi-colon or a full-stop, depending upon the length of the pause. It is no longer necessary to use as many commas as Charles Dickens did. Sentences are now usually shorter and simpler, too. The rule is to use punctuation marks when they make the meaning clear - otherwise don't. An excellent small book on punctuation is G. V. Carey's *Mind the Stop* (revised edn, Pelican, 1976).

Spelling
Use a dictionary. (For those who can't spell, J. Krevisky and J. L. Linfield's *The Awful Speller's Dictionary* (rev. by Oliver Stoner, Guiness, Enfield, UK, 1991) is a useful aid!)

Simplicity

Simplicity of expression does not mean being simple-minded. Use the simplest words that are accurate, as long as they are right for your purpose. Short sentences and short paragraphs usually work better, but there must be variety to avoid monotony.

Written language is also seen, so keep your writing visually uncluttered. White space is clean, crisp and attractive. Make use of it in the visual presentation of your work.

If you use four or five three-syllable words in a row, even if they are simple, commonly used words, your prose will look heavy or busy. Similarly, a majority of one-syllable words will look like a child's story.

Something to be aware of is the width of column in which your article will be printed. Very narrow columns make even medium-length paragraphs look depressingly long. If your work is going to be printed in such a format (check your target magazine), take extra care to break your article into short paragraphs.

Precision

Your aim is to communicate your thought as precisely as possible. You know the image or thought so well that it is easy to grab any word that will do the job of transferring the thought or image to the reader's mind - any word that will do, more or less. But unless the words are exact they will not be adequate to transmit the complete and correct image or idea. It is safer to assume the reader knows nothing, and to take considerable care in choosing the right word.

In English there are very few exact synonyms. There are many pairs, or even clusters, of words which mean almost the same thing - but not quite. So be precise. Use the word which conveys your meaning *exactly*. But, beware, any rule about the use of words is elastic. Although 'siblings' is precise and everyone knows what it means, it is too clinical, almost pedantic, when used in a non-technical context. Mostly, the longer, more casual 'brothers and sisters' is better.

While the language has to be exactly right, as close to perfect as you can get, to hold the readers, the words should not intrude. You want your reader to be engrossed in the story, not distracted by unusual words.

Avoid the sort of open-ended comparatives we see so much of in advertising, for example, 'We try harder'. Harder than whom? 'This toothpaste has 30% more such and such'. 30% more than what?

Repetition

Avoid disconcerting repetition of words. English has many words that sound and are spelt the same but have different meanings, for example, 'wax', meaning to grow, and also a polish; 'box', meaning to fight, and also a container. Do not use both of the pair in the same paragraph, on the same page, or even in the same short article.

Also avoid using within the same page words of the same sound, but different spelling and meaning, such as 'wears' and 'wares', also 'sight' and 'site', 'weight' and 'wait'. Then there are pairs of words such as 'wind' (that blows) and 'wind' (the clock). These, too, should not appear on the same page or even in the same article. Any of these echoes may be enough to make readers frown in puzzlement, and look back to see if they have read it correctly. It interrupts the comprehension of your meaning.

Numbers

Clarify large numbers. 'Nearly a thousand hectares' is more easily visualised than '913 hectares'. 'Four times the size of (a well-known) park' is even better. Use both if that clarifies understanding. If a concept seems abstract or likely to be difficult to understand, re-state it in different words.

Use 'number' when things are countable, and 'amount' when referring to a mass. Do not refer, as some television newsreaders often do, to 'the highest *amount* of road fatalities'.

Avoid technical terms when writing for a lay audience

This applies to any words that might be confusing to even one reader. Try to avoid anything that interrupts communication. If any alternative would be imprecise, yet you think some readers may be unfamiliar with the precise and necessary technical word, explain it with a simple definition, then continue without any suggestion of being patronising. For example, if you are writing about antique bronzes, explain the meaning of 'patina' (the greenish film produced by oxidation over time) the first time you mention it. Otherwise constant descriptions of it would waste words and become boring.

Use your own voice

Speak in your own voice, but sometimes you will have to slow down to keep your readers with you. You are familiar with your thoughts, give your readers time to tune into your thinking.

Write lean and clean

- Avoid qualifiers and wasted words. 'It's probably true to say that scones are undoubtedly a little less fattening than cake' means the same as 'Scones are less fattening than cake'.

These 'clutter' words are sometimes used for a good reason in conversation. If the speaker could be seen as threatening, or too-powerful, then 'clutter' words soften or weaken the message to a degree that the listener can take in the message without being intimidated.

This does not apply in writing. 'Clutter' words in print reduce your message to meaninglessness.

- Plain is better than fancy. 'To read' is better than 'to interact with print'.

- Do not use modifiers with words that cannot take modifiers, such as 'very unique' or 'slightly impossible'.

Quotes and dialogue

These are often used in non-fiction, and have many advantages. They break up the page visually by providing unexpected white spaces; they soften or humanise the article by bringing in another character. Readers are usually interested in learning someone else's thoughts and feelings. You, the writer, must be careful to introduce just those quotes that will affect the readers in the way you wish them to be affected.

- You can 'borrow' credentials by quoting from an authority to support an argument or generalisation.

- You can use a quote from a person you have interviewed for your article. This 'first-hand' quote will also support your argument. If this person, say, a woman, is quoted at length, then take the trouble to characterise her in some other way, too. Describe her, tell the readers a little about her, so that the readers feel they know her.

- Quotes from either of these sources can be used in other ways, too. Quotes often make an effective eye-catcher. They can also can be used to close an article with a succinct summary, or a wry comment. They can also be boxed as a side-bar.

- If you have a funny or startling quote, use it. If it is not suitable for use at the beginning or end of the article, write a special paragraph to stage it.

- Information gained from interviews is often best written as a mixture of direct and indirect speech, broken with description or other information.

- In non-fiction your reader must believe that what you write is fact. Therefore, quotes have to be reported exactly as they are spoken, or the sense and spirit of the statement paraphrased accurately.

If a speaker has 'uhmmed' and 'ahhed' and interrupted the conversation, it may be better for you to write a shorter, clearer version, then refer it to the speaker for permission to use it as a quotation. A tactful way is to show the cleaned-up version, or read it over the telephone, and ask for confirmation that that is what was said. It is likely that the interviewee won't realise that you have cleaned up the prose. (See Chapter 7 for more on interviewing.)

Anecdotes

These lend weight to your argument in just the same way that quotes, statistics, and description do. They have an additional value. Told with a light touch, anecdotes lighten your article, but keep them closely related to the point you want to prove. More than any other writing technique they are likely to get out of control, and you may be in danger of either losing your reader, or having your reader lose the thread of the story.

Keep anecdotes as brief as possible. A mid-way reference to the point you are supporting or a relevant generalisation may be needed to keep your reader on track.

STYLE

Style is simply the way *you* write. Whatever tips I give you here are merely suggestions to help you think of ways of improving your style, because, above all else, your style is you - not me, not your favourite writer, no one but you.

We all have the same material to work with - words. We each try to fashion our vocabulary of words into a well-fitting, stylish garment that is specially designed for its user and its purpose - ourselves and the article we are writing.

As we progress, we all work at improving our understanding of the material we have to work with, and our skill in designing ways of combining words for special effects. We extend our vocabulary, and we read good non-fiction writers, not to copy but to observe and learn from their success.

Find out what other writers are doing, how they are writing, what they are doing to achieve certain effects, but do what you want to do, write what you want to write. Be sensitive to what is happening around you. Don't be afraid to change, don't be afraid to be curious, to be innovative, but above all *be you.*

Of all the ingredients that make a writer, most can be learned, copied, restyled, or changed. Only one ingredient is a one-off - your own essential essence. You are an original. There never has been and there never will be another like you, so exploit and enjoy your individuality.

By paying attention to the points discussed below I was able to make my writing stronger, smoother, more evocative, more gripping, and, I hope, more enjoyable for my readers. If you find the suggestions helpful, great. If you find them of no use at all, ignore them. You will know if they are wrong for you. Take only what you want.

Viewpoint

If you write as you speak, chattily and comfortably, your writing will have the rhythm of spoken language. Such a style will give you several bonuses.

It will enable you to reach naturally for support material (for illustrations, anecdotes, etc).

It will help you to get words down on paper. If you decide after the first draft is written that the work calls for more formality, then you can adjust it in the next draft.

If you use the conversational first and second person - 'I' (the writer) talking to 'you' (the reader) with an occasional shift to 'we', you will come across to the reader as you are, without the need to intrude. It is much softer and friendlier, than the stiff 'one'.

There are alternatives you will sometimes choose. You will sometimes use the third person exclusively, keeping yourself out of the story - for example, if you tell the story of someone or something remote from your reader's experience, such as battle horror or the survivors' recourse to cannibalism after a shipwreck in Antarctica.

Match words and meaning

In deciding how you are going to write, what you are going to write, and for whom you are going to write, you are choosing a mood, a manner, a voice. Of course, you will change your mood and manner to suit the material and the market. With each article you will choose the proper voice to use when telling this story to that audience.

Your aim is to cast a spell upon the readers, to have them travel with you. To do this, you, the writer, should not intrude, for if you do you will break the spell.

Sometimes the story calls for readers to be jolted. This is best done by suddenly using inappropriate language, something that immediately gives notice of a change of mood mid-journey. The skill comes in knowing when.

The mood or tone will vary with the material, but they can be described in four broad categories.

1 Objective or totally detached. You offer no personal opinion, you keep yourself and the readers out of the story. You carefully avoid bias in the words you use. You describe things and events as accurately as you can, then you let the readers decide for themselves. Work such as a police report, or a studiedly impersonal report of an event, political happening, civic ceremony, or new medical technique, may be written in this detached, objective way. Sometimes, indeed, if the story is shocking or impressive enough, it will succeed in evoking deeper emotions than less objective writing would.

2 Subjective. The writer and the readers are involved, but usually not in a deeply emotional way. Most articles, including how-tos, travel reports, and reviews, are written in this mood.

3 Sympathetic. You ask the readers to feel sorry for someone - a third person, or group. This works best if you feel sympathy for the people in the story, and it shows. These are the stories about how a handicapped child made good, how a family coped with the murder of one of their number, how a community is helping its down-and-out citizens rehabilitate themselves, how a new mayor is encouraging citizens to brighten up their neighbourhood, etc. It remains reportage, but with feeling. You may also ask the reader to share anger, outrage, satisfaction, pride, or amusement.

4 Empathetic. 'Empathy' is defined as the power of projecting your personality into, and so fully understanding, a person

or object of contemplation. Stories told in this tone are often on the same subject matter as those told in a sympathetic tone, but they are more moving because you, the writer, have been there, and you invite the reader to share the experience. The measure of the success of these articles, which at their best are the most successful of all, depends upon the tenderness with which you can involve the reader in the experience without sinking into sentimentality. Any hint of feeling sorry for yourself is fatal.

These categories cannot be hard and fast, there are grey edges. Try to match the tone of the language you use to the feeling you wish to evoke in the reader. This is easy. We do it in real life all the time: you visit your elderly mother to help her pack for a hospital visit, and for that occasion, with that person, your mother, you use one tone of voice; you talk to a small boy kicking leaves in the park; you introduce a newcomer to your neighbours; you speak to the manager of the shop where you were sold ill-fitting curtains. To all of these people you use a different, and quite distinct, tone of voice. With your mother you would use a tone of encouragement; to the boy, perhaps light-hearted friendliness; one of welcome to the newcomer; calm conviction that you had not been served well to the shop manager.

A little thought as to your purpose will enable you to use the correct tone in your story, too. The tone must be consistent throughout the article, or the message will become confused.

Music-pattern or harmony

There are no good or bad sounds; there are no wrong or right words. The words and their sounds have to be chosen to fit the place where you want to use them, the purpose for which you want to use them, and for the audience you want to reach and affect.

There must be balance and harmony in the shape of the

words in the sentence, and the sentences in the piece of writing; and there must be balance and harmony in the whole story.

The sound of the words, and how they operate together, contribute to the quality of your story. The mood of the piece, and its meaning dictates the appropriate music-pattern (or rhythm). Usually if you write as you speak, the music-pattern comes automatically. But sometimes, if you want a special effect, you have to deliberately plan it with the use of forms such as parallel construction, alliteration, etc.

Sound

Although it is not a good idea for individual words to stand out - they distract the reader from the meaning - the situation is quite different with the overall sound or music. If the sound is memorable, it is more likely that the thought, the message, will be remembered.

A light touch will work with almost any subject. Even with a sad story, where tears, not laughter, will be evoked, subtlety will be more effective than exaggeratedly tragic tones. Treat your readers and your subjects with respect, but don't take yourself too seriously. You are a writer, an interpreter, a bearer of messages, a teller of tales. You are not God.

Many people have an instinctive ear for words. If you don't have that inner ear, read your work aloud. Listen for: words that don't sound well together, words that trip the tongue, words that are stridently not onomatopoeic (where the sound echoes the meaning), words that are so strong or heavy that they detract from the idea or feeling that you are striving to convey. Remember it is not only notes that make the music but the intervals between, so space your words according to their weight.

Take notice of how other writers, such as in books by my favourite author, Lawrence Durrell, achieve a distinctive sound (especially the Alexandria Quartet).

Hear the words

The differences in weight and strength of words affect the patterns of written language. Even in writing that is not meant to be read aloud, words have aural, as well as visual, weight. Watch for the following.

- Alliteration. In prose this is often irritating. 'The wailing wind' or 'The whining wind' are both attention-getters, and that may be just what you want to do. But 'The whining winter wind' is just too much!

  Be careful, too, with constructions such as 'pushing shelves'. The repetitive 'sh' draws attention to itself, so the readers *see* the words and *hear* the intrusive, repeated sound, and this might lead them from the story you are telling.

- Words which do not flow, perhaps because of the awkward sound of the last syllable of one word against the first syllable of the following word, for example, 'fir*st* *st*rike', 'dru*gged* *g*old-miner', etc., though 'rugged gold-miner' is all right – because the pronunciation of the final 'ed' in rugged as a separate syllable makes for a different balance of sound.

Though the words must be correct, they must be almost transparent. The *words* must be so perfect that they lead readers directly to the meaning, and do not themselves distract readers by any oddity, unusualness, or alliterative sound which does not fit the context.

Dress to suit the occasion

Some subjects, some markets, some story-types, call for leisurely, discursive writing. Others call for tight, fact-packed writing. Short does not mean easy. It is very difficult to cram a 500-word article full of information without it looking like a shopping list. But it can be done. Organise your information precisely, know exactly what you want to achieve, and include nothing else.

Short sentences are best. They are simplest, clearest, cleanest. But they should not *all* be short, nor should they all have the same construction. Both the length of sentences and their shape should vary widely for it is this variety that provides the melody.

Whether your article is to be formal or informal, use language, sentence construction and references that can readily be understood by your readers. Writing is generally slightly more formal than speech, but the stiffness of very formal language is often not necessary nor suitable. Informal language is used in most general-interest magazines and middle-of-the-road specialist magazines.

The difference in the language used in the various daily papers reflects their editors' perception of the differing education levels of their readers. Casual language is sometimes suitable, particularly if the writer and the readers belong to a homogeneous group (for example, when you are writing for a house journal). The extremely casual, almost colloquial, language used in magazines and newspaper columns aimed at specific groups of younger readers (rock-music fans or motorbike riders), is usually designed to make those readers feel that they belong to a special group.

Otherwise, avoid slang, jargon and colloquialisms, except in direct speech and for special effects. If they creep in, don't worry too much. In a few years some of the slang of today will have become respectable.

Pace your prose to match your story

The movement of your words, sentences and paragraphs should fit the actions and events that are unfolded. A reasoned discussion would need medium to long sentences. A race or an argument would need to be told in shorter, more staccato sentences. An accident, a disaster, or a fight could be described effectively in very short sentences. Look for examples of this in your reading.

Watch the use of adverbs, for they tend to slow down a sentence, to weaken it and draw it out. They can give an effect of thoughtfulness, dreaminess or tedium. If you want the story to move slowly and steadily, then use adverbs copiously; the slow pace works well for children's bedtime stories.

To keep a story moving, use more specific verbs instead of a vague verb plus an adverb. For example, 'He dawdled' (or 'staggered', or 'shuffled', or 'wandered') is better because these are each more specific (it depends what exactly you want to convey) than 'He walked slowly' 'She looked at it carefully' is not as exact as 'She peered at it', or 'She pored over it', 'She examined it', or 'She squinted at it'.

Words convey more than facts

Be aware that many words are emotion-laden. Use such words only when you want to communicate the weight of emotion. But don't be too cold-blooded, either. Your writing is you. If you want to evoke emotion in the reader, you too must invest some feeling.

Most of your thoughts, and particularly those of your opening, should be expressed as a positive statement, rather than negative. State what is, what should be, what can happen, instead of what is not, what should not be, and what cannot happen. The positive appeals, the negative repels.

It is more positive to be 'pro' something than 'anti' its opposite. This is particularly important in titles and slogans. For example, when the debate on abortion began, the two opposing sides were known as the 'pro-abortion' lobby and the 'anti-abortion' lobby. The anti-abortionists quickly saw that the name of their side of the argument had a negative sound and would inspire negative feelings rather than active support, so they began, instead, to use the name 'pro-life' for their movement. 'Life' is a word carrying very powerful emotions – all of them positive. The combined word 'pro-life' is clearly more attractive than 'pro-abortion'. The group supporting abortion could hardly call their argument 'anti-life'; 'pro-death' is even worse. This group now seem to have settled for 'pro-choice' in an effort to retain the positive suffix 'pro-'. 'Choice' is a positive word, but it has none of the strong emotions that 'life' has. So in the war of words, at least, the 'pro-life' movement is a clear winner.

In our culture, words like mother, child, love, are so emotion-laden that poets, who use words with infinite care, avoid them. They want their expressed *thought* to evoke emotion, not the words themselves. All writers must heed this.

An extreme example, 'orphan', is emotion-laden, but 'motherless' is even heavier in emotion, even though the condition is less serious – the child may still have a living father.

'She felt stifled as the crowd moved restlessly around her' is fairly neutral, but not quite. 'She felt breathless as the crowd seethed around her' suggests menace. 'Seethed' as a description of crowd movement implies intent. The feminine subject is important because females are, on average, shorter than males, so a woman would be seen more readily as being stifled or breathless in a crowd. If you had already established your subject as a tall man (and unless you had stated otherwise, by implication that would suggest taller than all women and most men), then neither sentence would evoke feelings of danger, threat or even discomfort.

Use words as tools to evoke the thought and feeling that you want your reader to experience.

Be versatile

Practise writing in different styles until you find the voice that is right for you.

Give no offence

Be careful not to use stereotypes with regard to such things as race, sex, age, job, etc. An easy guide is to avoid descriptions which belittle or unfairly stereotype any person or group of people.

Though today Aborigines, Negroes and other dark-skinned people often prefer to call themselves black people, be aware that over past centuries implications of the adjective 'black' (for example, black-hearted villain; bad guys always wear black hats; witches wear black; blackmail; blacklist; black for mourning clothes, hearse; painting things black, for depicting things in a bad light) have carried over to attitudes toward dark-skinned people. Awareness of the history of the dichotomy between black and white, darkness and light, will prevent you from falling unthinkingly into the trap of stereotyping with regard to skin-colour.

You will offend a large proportion of your readers if you depict women in roles suggesting weakness or submissiveness, and as less educated, less intelligent, less capable, or less successful. Differences in our society do exist, not always because of gender differences. You are a factual writer, so do not hesitate to tell it 'like it is', but in the telling be aware that over 50 per cent of your readers are going to resent any implication that such a division in society is fair and based on inherent gender differences.

Similarly, until recently women have been referred to, in English at least, as belonging to 'mankind'. This attitude has moulded our language to such an extent that we have no singular pronoun that refers to a male *or* a female. This is a situation which no writer can avoid. You have to make a decision

- to twist your sentences around into passive tense (I usually choose not to do this because I believe that it leads to loss of strength and clarity);

- to accept the present limitations of English, and use the feminine and masculine pronouns in an even-handed manner (that is, do not always refer to the boss or higher-status person as masculine, and the lower-status person as feminine),
- to use the plural pronoun 'they' (which can lead to some ambiguity),
- in formal articles, where it may sometimes be permissible, to use the conglomerate he/she, her/him, etc.

You must make your own choice, depending upon the context. In this, as in other difficult areas, your writing is you. You must do what is right for you.

Other common stereotypes refer to such things as height, weight or age. For example, you may wish to refer to an old man, and describe him as a stooped, grey-haired man. Be aware that your character is a man first, whether or not he is stooped and whether or not he has grey hair are additional pieces of descriptive information. Not all old men are either stooped or grey-haired.

As a writer you must keep up-to-date with current attitudes. Whatever might have been the case in the early 1900s, today a sixty-year-old woman does not consider herself old. She is likely to be slim, attractive, fashionably dressed, and doing a full-time paid job. Many sixty-year-old women in our society do have children who have children. Nevertheless, they are, firstly, women. Only incidentally, and if it is relevant to the story, are their additional roles of wife or widow, spinster, divorcee, mother and grandmother, worth mentioning.

Verbs

Use transitive verbs whenever you can: action verbs are better than static ones. 'To be' is the dullest, as it doesn't move.

Use a 'doing' (action) verb if at all possible. Writing 'The trophy *sat* on the table' rather than 'The trophy *was* on the table', suggests some action, some life.

Of course, it is even more effective when some movement is actually taking place, and you can state that the girls *hit* the ball, *banged* the door, *rushed* or *tumbled* into a room (rather than *came* into it), or that the tired boy *dropped* his satchel, *flung* his books, or *slumped* into a chair.

Use active instead of passive voice most of the time. Active voice has more authority. People who are not sure of what they are saying try to bluff by using passive voice. It shows. 'Molly pushed the boy roughly from the room, shielding his trembling body by leaning on the door' is more lively, more easily and vividly visualised than 'The boy was pushed roughly from the room by Molly. His trembling body was shielded by the door she was leaning on'. But in this, too, you need variety. Passive voice allows periods of calm, a lull in the activity.

Avoid tautology

Listen to television with a new interest. Enjoy listening for such examples of over-kill as 'descend down', 'revert back', 'long-lasting durability'. You will hear about people who 'receive their weekly pay every Friday', and those who are 'immortalised in stone and live forever'.

Do not use clichés or platitudes

An example, of a cliché is 'white as snow'. Avoid platitudes - obvious ideas, many of which have come down to us as proverbs such as 'The early bird catches the worm', 'All that glitters is not gold', 'Too many cooks spoil the broth'.

Onomatopoeic words

These are words whose sound resembles or echoes their meaning, such as hiss, mutter, thunder, rumble. Heroes have strong-sounding names for good reason. In *Wuthering Heights* Emily Brontë chose to call her wild, black, isolated hero Heathcliff - a name which echoed those characteristics. The heroes in romantic novels are likely to have names like Brett, Roderick, Chet, Warwick (notice the hard consonants), as they are hard, strong, outdoor types. Simon, Paul, Martin are more likely to be thoughtful, quieter heroes. Fiction writers use the sound of names to help characterise their 'people'.

Show, don't tell

Treat your readers with respect. Don't reach conclusions for them. Don't tell them how to feel, what judgement to make. Just give them the evidence, and let them make up their own minds.

Don't *tell* readers that a lawyer is busy, *show* them the lawyer at work, with phones ringing and people waiting. Don't tell readers that a child is beautiful, describe the clear skin and shining eyes so that they can see for themselves.'

Exercises

1 Evoke a vivid visual image of each of the following by writing a descriptive paragraph using all five senses (sight, hearing, touch, taste and smell) in each description:

- a circus
- a deserted house
- a picnic spot near a river
- a child waiting alone at a street intersection
- a dancer
- a wind-blown tree.

Put these aside for a time, and go on with exercise 2.

2 Take these ten nouns: golfer, waitress, dancer, schoolboy, artist, kangaroo, room, chair, surfer, car, and pair them with these ten adjectives: sleek, angry, stable, sturdy, old, tatty, weary, untidy, enthusiastic, dejected. Now write a sentence for each pair without using either of the given words, but in a way that makes the concept clear and without stereotyping: for example, if I paired 'dancer' and 'weary' I might write: Kate flopped on the chair to the left of the stage, and began massaging her aching feet.

3 Try to improve the writing of that first draft of Exercise 1. For each example:

- Look at the paragraph arrangement. Are the sentences arranged in the most logical order?
- Are the sentences themselves correct? Are they of varied construction and length?
- Are the words used the best, the most exact, the most vivid and alive?
- Would the sentences be improved by cutting?
- Do the words sound well together? Do the sentences read well together? Make any changes you think will improve the paragraphs, but keep your first draft - and then compare the two.

6

WRITERS WRITE

Everyone who wants to write, can. To write well takes talent, creativity, and, for most of us, consistent writing practice. Beginning writers often find it difficult to accept that they have all the talent and creativity they could possibly need, that their unwillingness to write consistently is the cause of their high failure rate.

Even experienced writers complain about 'writer's block', and many beginning writers are frustrated by their seeming inability to put their ideas onto paper. In this chapter we will look at ways of writing that will almost certainly remove any writer's block once and for all.

'Talent' means a natural ability, a disposition for anything, a mental endowment. You would not be reading this book if you did not love words and reading, if you did not have more than a passing interest in putting your thoughts on paper. Therefore, you do have sufficient talent to become a successful writer.

'Creativity' means having the ability to create; it is in everyone who has within them any spark of enthusiasm or joy in living. A few years ago only artists and children were widely acknowledged as being creative. The business world has now recognised the value of imagination and creative thinking in entrepreneurial activities, and most people accept the concept that they are, or can be, creative.

If we have the talent and creativity to write, then what is stopping us from writing? Perhaps we are inhibited, blocked, self-conscious, or shy? If we were all creative as children, where did the creativity go?

It didn't go anywhere, it is still there, ready to be tapped, ready to be encouraged to flow. Rigid schooling, unimaginative work practices, or harsh criticism, may have dammed up our creativity, preventing it from flowing normally, *but it is still there.* All we have to do is to encourage it. One of the easiest ways of encouraging creativity, of opening the flood-gates, is to relax, and to find ways to relieve the stress in our lives.

THE TWO SIDES OF OUR BRAIN

Each of us has a brain divided into two halves - the left and right sides. The two halves have millions of inter-connectors, but each side of the brain has a different function, each side has its own way of dealing with the world.

The right side of the brain is the emotional intuitive side. It is sometimes referred to as the unconscious self. It is nearly, but not wholly, the same as the 'id' of Freudian psychology. This side of the brain is the artistic side. It is visual, imaginative, creative, inventive, capricious, lazy, even indolent. This side of the brain dreams dreams and spins tales, spawns brilliant ideas, and hatches hare-brained schemes (but is not very good at organising how to carry them out!).

The left side of the brain is the intellectual or rational side. It is often referred to as our conscious self; this term is somewhat similar to Freud's concept of the 'ego'. The left side of the brain is strong on common sense, restraint, rational behaviour, and discipline. This side of the brain controls our activities as a craftsperson, an editor, or a critic.

In ordinary day-to-day living we use both sides of our brain continuously, and usually alternately in rapid succession. For example, our right brain might spark the idea of looking to see what the new shop across the street is selling. Our left brain tells us that we don't really need anything. The right brain reminds us that it is our nephew's birthday next week. We respond to the idea by moving to cross the street. Our left brain takes over to guard us from a possible traffic accident. At the shop we are charmed by a brilliantly displayed toy in the window. Our right brain decides to buy it; the left brain chides us – it costs far too much, and is really more of a girl's toy than a boy's. The right brain decides that unisex is the way to go, and, besides, the boy's small sister will also enjoy it, therefore it is really a toy for two children; looked at from that point of view it is not expensive at all, positively a bargain!

We all use both sides of our brains. Both sides have work to do. The balance of the alternating dominance of one or other side of the brain will determine what sort of person we are and what sort of life we lead.

We can write more productively if we learn to use both sides of the brain in a special way. To write freely and fluently, to write whenever we want and whatever we want, we must learn to balance our right-brain and left-brain activities, by using each side separately, not alternately in quick succession, in the way our education and our lifestyle have accustomed us to do, but by quite deliberately choosing to use first the right side, then the left side. As writers we must guard against letting these two selves act against each other in a competitive way. We must know when to let the artist have the upper hand, and when to let the craftsperson take over.

A story rises in the unconscious mind, and should be encouraged to flow freely. The essence of the story and its theme arise in the right brain. And the right brain should be permitted to finish its work as artist, creator, and spinner of tales, before the left brain undertakes its work of critic and editor. The job for the left brain is to work on the creation from the right brain and to make it more readable – but not yet!

Writing is words on paper. Writing is not an engaging story you thought up when you couldn't sleep; writing is not a fabulous adventure you had when you were a child; writing is not an amusing anecdote to tell the family at dinner. Writing is none of these things until it is written down – it must be words on paper.

After it is written we call on the left brain to choose the most appropriate words; to shape the story in the most effective way; to decide whether the story should be pruned or expanded; to check and re-check spelling, punctuation, etc. It is important that the commonsense editor or critic takes over only after the creator has produced and put down on paper the free flow of ideas expressed in words.

Compare this with how Sally, a beginning writer, usually writes. She has an idea, and begins to write. Then she stops, often before she has completed one sentence, as her left brain starts to edit: 'Is that the best way of putting it? Perhaps I could start the story somewhere else?' So she starts somewhere else, but tries to correct that first sentence as she goes, too. The result is that dozens of beginnings are made, but never an ending, and very rarely even a middle. Then after weeks of frustrating work, with nothing to show for the effort, Sally decides that perhaps it wasn't such a good idea after all. She waits until a better idea comes along. It does. Her right brain becomes active, and she starts another story. But because she again lets her left brain interfere before its time, the same sequence of actions prevent her from finishing her story.

Make the right brain's job easy

- Dare to be idle. Imagination works best when you are not pressed for time. Dawdle; allow yourself the luxury of sometimes just pottering. If big ideas don't come, use little ideas. The big ideas will come when you are relaxed before a fire, or walking beside the ocean, or doing some mindless automatic task like washing the dishes or the car.

- Develop a child-like eye. Learn to really look at things, see them in all their detail. This applies to your other senses, too.

- Dare to write the truth as you see it. Don't write what you think other people might want; write what is right for you. You can only be original when you are uniquely yourself.

- Give yourself permission to write badly. If in this competitive world you have always been a success, you might find it difficult to write for fear of writing less than well. *It doesn't matter.* You can write badly. No one need know. Your writing can remain private, until you want it otherwise. If fear of writing badly is stopping you from writing, let go of the fear. Go ahead, write badly. Do it deliberately, then you will know that it doesn't matter. You can write, then screw up the pages and fill the wastepaper basket. Or if there is anything good at all in what you write, you can revise and rewrite it until it is as good as you can make it, until it is something you won't want to throw in the wastepaper basket.

- Write early each morning - before speaking, before reading, before turning on the radio. Write in a half-awake state for 3–10 minutes. Write anything that is in your mind. Write of a half-remembered dream; write of yesterday's activities; write of a present joy, or a recent sadness; write of a new friend, or an old car - anything. Remember, this writing is for your eyes only.

  If you do this exercise each morning, even if you must wake earlier than usual to do so, you will find that it develops your writing muscle; it gets your creative juices flowing. Even better, it will develop a habit of writing so that you will have it as a ready weapon to deal with the infamous writer's block if ever it should bother you.

  The late Dorothea Brande recommended this exercise in her wonderful book *Becoming a Writer* (Papermac, Macmillan, London, 1934; republished 1983). The prolific novelist John Braine, in his laudatory foreword, gave her tip credit for 'unblocking' the novel he was then struggling to write.

- Develop the writing habit. The morning writing will help, and soon you will be able to write whenever you want. Though your morning exercises are just that - exercises - they may contain ideas and snippets that lead to the day's work. If so, add to it freely. Remember you are still giving your right brain full control.

  Many writers write a regular journal to keep up the practice of free, uninhibited writing. When you are thoroughly established in the writing habit, and write on your 'public' writing every day, there is no need to write in your journal daily. It is important not to feel pressured. Be kind to yourself. This should be a time of relaxation, of inner exploration. On re-reading you will find that it is a source of ideas you may not have recognised at the time of writing.

- Write truly of your feelings - not only when they are violent or heart-rending. Quiet contentment, even boredom, is just as valid. Write from where you are now, not from memory; write as you feel now. Only write cheerfully if you feel cheerful. If you are lonely and depressed, write about that.

Put the right side of your brain to work

- Tell stories, don't just use words. Relate anecdotes in fiction style, with full regard to pacing; allow pauses between periods of action. Tell your story to share with others something of your life experience or imagination. Be generous. Tell your story as if to a friend, even an imaginary one. In non-fiction you must write what really happened, but add depth by adding your views, speculating on possible results, and providing opinions from experts.

- Let the thoughts flow. Trust yourself to put down one thought after the other. Don't make judgements yet about your thoughts or the words or the pattern of the story, or anything else. If the beginning sentence doesn't come, leave a space and go on to the next paragraph. Don't worry about having a complete story, write what is in you, write what you know *now*. If you realise as you write that you need more information or more detail, just write that in (that you need to see so-and-so, look up such-and-such, or get this or that information). Try to put in as many of the bones of the story as possible, particularly the thesis and, if you know it, the conclusion.

- Be precise, not poetic; be accurate, not literary, in the words you use to express your thoughts. Don't worry if the information reads like a list. Editing comes later. Be truthful, exact and detailed. For vivid imagery use concrete physical details about colour, scents, length of shadows, textures, etc.

- Show, don't tell. Tell your readers what to see, don't tell them what to think. Describe in finest detail, for example, how a woman looks and what she does, but don't say she is fascinating, brave, etc. That is an opinion your readers may arrive at after you have provided them with the evidence.

- When you write, don't talk. During this creative stage of your work don't tell anyone about your idea, or even that you are writing. Your unconscious mind does not discriminate between talking and writing. If you tell your story in any form, it will be a finished action, and your mind will not go on working on it. You will lose interest. Talk about your project only after the first draft is down on paper, and then only to people who will encourage you.

- Don't be too shy to try. Write with enthusiasm and joy, or dogged determination. No matter how poor your first effort is, it can be improved. The bonus is that the actual creation, even if not itself successful, adds to your skill. The next time you will write better.

Now for the left side of the brain

- Establish rapport. Readers will like and trust you as a writer if you put them at ease, and explain in an easy conversational tone anything that needs explaining. Know your audience, and use the right tone and language for those readers in relation to your particular subject.

- Make the readers care. The great oral storytellers and chroniclers of the past used their personalities to engage the attention of their listening audiences, but if a story wasn't interesting people didn't continue to listen. (Can you imagine propping yourself against a restaurant piano and holding the attention of a crowd with your discourse?) As well as the intrinsic interest of the matter, listeners are held by the voice, personality and face of a speaker, and to some extent by good manners. With writing, all you have to grip the reader with is your skill in evoking images and emotion by words on paper.

- Be clear. Before readers can understand what you are saying, *you* have to know what you are saying. It is your responsibility to see that readers do not lose their way from your eye-catcher and thesis, through the tale you have to tell, to your summing-up and conclusion.

- Be concise. Don't waste words, but never sacrifice clarity for brevity. Dense prose can often be heavy going. Allow breathing space between ideas.

- Write precisely of one thing, to illustrate the many. It is more immediate and interesting to read of one particular four-year-old boy than of small boys in general, to learn about one well-delineated chemical engineering student than students in general. Readers can build up their own images of a whole neglected town from your vivid description of one ramshackle building in a run-down street.

- Be even-handed. Everyone likes to see fair play. If you criticise somebody or something, either take responsibility for the criticism or name the critic. Even in reviews, and evaluative articles where you are obliged to give your opinion, give the opposing side some space. It often advances your own argument if you outline the opposition's case as well.

- Keep a narrow focus. Don't waver from the point you wish to make.

- Build up to your climax. To retain the readers' interest, the body of the story must be presented with all the dramatic flair you can muster. For example, if an earthquake is about to destroy a town, make sure that the reader hears the ground rumble first.

- Organise the material logically. Use one of the patterns from Chapter 3, or some other effective and persuasive form. At this stage there will be blanks. That's all right. At least after getting it into order you can see what extra work you have to do.

Here is a quick and easy plan for shaping an article.

1 Obtain five large sheets of paper.

2 Divide each of the first four pages into four equal parts by ruling three horizontal lines across.

3 Page 1: Label the top section 'Title', the next section 'Eye-catcher', the next 'Thesis', and the lowest one 'Why the Reader Should Care, and My Credentials'.

4 Page 2: Label the top section 'Point 1'. The three other sections of that page are for three pieces of supporting evidence.

5 Pages 3 and 4: Label these in a similar manner for 'Point 2' and 'Point 3'.

6 Page 5: Divide this into two. Label the top half 'Summary' and the lower half 'Close'.

With this plan before you, you can see at a glance what you need in order to make yours a well-organised article. Fill the planning sheets straight from your first draft, the one you wrote straight off without conscious thinking or organising. You can re-write it into the plan, or you can 'cut-and-paste' from your free draft onto the plan.

Almost certainly you will be able to fill in most of the sections straight away. You will know what you want to say, and how you know about it, so you will be able to fill in the 'Thesis' and 'Credentials'.

Then see how many points with supporting evidence your first free-writing draft included. From them fill in the sections for the three points (from weakest to strongest). If you have more points, just add more sheets. Start filling in whatever support material you have, ensuring that the supporting evidence clearly supports the point.

Give the project a working title straight away; fill in the 'Title' section. Having a working title labels the article in your mind, enabling you to focus your thoughts.

As you keep thinking, write in additional points and evidence, and weigh up which anecdotes would be most convincing. At this point you will be able to see what additional research you will need in order to round out the article.

With the plan completed, use it as your work-sheet to write the article.

That wasn't difficult, was it? All it takes is some thought, a simple plan, and then some action to make the plan work.

Exercises

1 Do the free-writing exercise every morning upon awakening - or at some other time when you are relaxed and free of interruptions. Write freely for 3-10 minutes. Write whatever comes into your mind. Just express the ideas and the thoughts, don't worry about the words. Don't edit, or try to improve your work. Don't even read it over until you have done the exercise every day for a week.

2 Write your proposed article as fully and freely as you can from what you know. Don't look up notes, or try to organise the article, just write and keep on writing until you have written all you know on the subject.

3 Take your free-writing version of your article and shape it into logical form. Use either the five-page method outlined, or some other organisation which will suit the material.

7

RESEARCH

You are now well advanced in the production of your article.

You have decided upon the idea, and focused the subject until you know exactly what point you want to make.

You have examined all the likely markets, and decided exactly which publication your article is right for.

You have studied the articles printed in your target magazine thoroughly until you feel confident that you know the tone that suits that editor and the taste of the readers.

You have done a free-writing draft of your article, and then you have shaped it roughly into a logical form, perhaps by using the five-sheet method.

You have ascertained what else you need to fill out the story. Further research may be necessary, and perhaps some interviews.

Later, you will do further work on the article only after you receive a go-ahead from an editor. But now proceed with the article idea you have thought about for so long.

All productive writers of short non-fiction read everything that in any way touches on their interests. Their interests constantly expand. In this way they keep up-to-date with their current interests, and are forever adding new subjects.

A broad variety of interests makes it easier to adapt rapidly to any change in the market-place. But wide reading cannot take the place of specific research for a particular article.

Most articles need research of one kind or another. The more informative, factual article requires specific, detailed and up-to-date information, perhaps statistics, and perhaps interviews with experts. These are the 'nuts and bolts' of the article.

Editors need solid supportable information, specific, useful facts that can be checked if necessary; editors insist on identifiable sources, not quotes from anonymous characters; editors demand accuracy with details such as names, addresses, dates, times, and costs.

If the facts are useful for readers to know, then these facts will be interesting. If you are recommending a holiday in a snow resort in summer, then the main points of your article might be the vastly lower costs applying during the off-season, and that the snow country has different attractions during summer; it would be essential that you list the summer prices as compared to the winter prices. It might also be relevant for you to give comparable prices for a beach holiday compared to a snow-resort summer holiday, as well as the names and addresses and contact phone numbers for booking those ski lodges open in summer. The different options should be explained, for example, you should specify those lodges where children are welcome, since most families with young children spend their summer holidays together. The air, rail and/or bus fares from the capital cities could be mentioned, particularly any packages designed to attract off-season visitors.

If the main thrust of your article is to extol in prose and pictures the beautiful wildflowers and bushwalks available in the snow country in summer, then slip the mundane but necessary information in with style - or arrange it in a sidebar.

Such details are not needed for all articles. The profile article usually requires research of published material for a comprehensive understanding of the background of the subject, plus one or more personal interviews.

Even nostalgic and personal-experience articles require research to refresh your memory of contemporary events (what the world was like at the time). Nearly all articles benefit from the inclusion of anecdotes closely related to the point you are making.

Always give the authority for your facts. If it is a technical article the editor and the readers will be more impressed by an authoritative source than by your opinion.

Don't confuse your readers. If you wish to draw conclusions after giving information from a variety of sources, indicate clearly that you are doing this. Sometimes it is better just to give the information and to allow readers to draw their own conclusions. If you wish to disagree with the authority you are quoting, say so.

You can write an article on a subject you know little about, but you will then need to do some background reading to get the general feel of the subject, specialised research, interviews with experts and read relevant literature. It will take time for you to organise all of this.

THE FIRST STEP IN RESEARCH

Take time to think where the information is located, and how you can get it.

You may decide to write an article on severely intellectually handicapped children, making a particular point of the strain that looking after such children places on their families. You have had no training or personal experience in the field, but you do know a family with such a child, and you have observed the difficulties the family endures.

The members of that family would probably be your principal resource. Check with them first to see whether they would be happy to share their experience with you. They may also be able to introduce you to other families in a similar situation, who could provide additional evidence, anecdotes, etc. But that wouldn't be enough. You would also have to contact the government departments and other agencies which provide health and educational care for the children and support care for such families.

Your article would need to touch on historic changes in care-giving, and changing community attitudes, and also to look at what support would be ideal, or at least what the present government social workers and the subject families believe to be ideal, and whether the government departments have plans to increase their level of support. Depending on the length of your article you might also survey community support groups, and comment on ways developed by other communities, here and overseas, dealing with this problem.

THREE VITAL QUESTIONS

As you become a professional writer you will realise that there are three questions related to research that you must consider in relation to each article-idea.

1 Do I know where to get the research material, and is it available to me?

2 If interviews are necessary or desirable, do I know precisely who to interview, and are they willing to be interviewed?

3 Even if the answers to the above questions are positive, is the article going to be economically feasible? Is doing the research and conducting the interviews going to cost more in time or money than is reasonable in relation to the payment I will receive for the article?

Research includes gathering the data you need from relevant sources, and includes interviews, and can be divided into material research and people research. For any article you will probably need both. Multiple sources are likely to result in a richer, rounder article; one source will suggest others.

Travel is often helpful, too. Visit the place you are writing about, if that is possible. It will give you a firm visual and mental framework for developing your article. The framework should not be obvious, but if it is not there the article will seem flimsy.

WHERE TO START

The most convenient place to start researching is with yourself. How much do you know about the subject? Think deeply. Is there more information available in your memory which you can use to fill the gaps still remaining in your article? What about your friends? Ask other people if they know anything about the subject. Don't talk about the story itself, just ask for information.

WHEN TO STOP

Some non-fiction, such as history, is often based on researching every aspect of the subject exhaustively, then gathering together all the material and presenting it logically. Obviously, this is very time-consuming, and it leaves the writer open to a common malaise – researching and researching and researching, researching for the love of researching, but never actually writing!

This method, while legitimate for history, is most often used when writing book-length non-fiction. For articles there is simply too much material on any subject; such a method leads to an amorphous mass of information, and a tremendous waste of a writer's most precious resource, time.

It is far better to follow the method outlined in previous chapters:

1 Decide what particular point you want to make about the subject – that is, the thesis of your article.

2 Pour out on paper all you currently know about that point.

3 Shape logically all you have freely written, and identify exactly what gaps you need to fill to make the article balanced and valid.

4 Direct your research in the particular direction needed to fill those gaps.

MATERIAL RESEARCH

- Once you have made the decision to be a writer you will need your own reference books. These are the most convenient research tools of all. Choose books in your own special areas; remember that second-hand books are cheap; look for those with information that will not date. Even if you have to check elsewhere for up-to-date information, you will have saved valuable time by doing the preliminary research in your own study.

- Spend a little time, and, if necessary, make some phone calls to find out just where the information is available. Go first to those places where most of the necessary information is easily available; for example, the State Library, State Archives, Land Titles Office, your local Council Chambers, your local library, local historical society, newspaper files (you will probably have to get permission in advance, and book a time) - newspapers are good for what was happening at the time, the weather, prices of commodities, etc., but never take a newspaper report as a true record unless you have evidence from some other source. Don't overlook university libraries, and university staff as expert and authoritative resources; state and federal government departments; your own federal and state members of parliament; recognised experts in the field (competent and qualified professionals are usually surprisingly helpful, and want nothing in return except courtesy, and perhaps a copy of the published article); local experts for local subjects; chambers of commerce, professional bodies and trade associations; private firms, most have staff willing to help you, particularly if it leads to publicity for their organisation (however, do be aware that their public relations officers are only interested in showing their employers in the best possible light). The yellow pages of phone books may lead you to firms or people who can help; they also list sporting associations, and public and private charities (once again beware of any figures unless they are on an audited balance sheet).

- In a library seek help from the reference librarians. Most librarians are an unbelievably generous source of help. They will steer you towards the best reference books, order books they don't have from other libraries on inter-library loan, search for out-of-the-way information, even give you a quick lesson on how to use their state-of-the-art computer/information terminals. Make yourself known to the librarians as a writer, ask what is the least busy time for you to seek their help – and cherish them!

- After you have collected the largest part of your material from your major resources, seek help from people there on where other material is available. Go back to your partly finished article. Make whatever changes the research made necessary, and see what else you need. Perhaps the rest of the information can be collected over the phone? If not, go to your next-most-likely source of research material. Try to avoid using resources which will take a lot of your time.

- When taking notes in a library, or indeed from any printed matter, be extravagant with paper. Write just *one* note on each sheet. Some writers use cards, and ordinary index cards are indeed the right size, and convenient for carrying in handbag or pocket. However, I come from a long line of Scottish forebears, and I found myself using the backs of cards. (This was a disaster as I often missed information; also the two pieces of research could be neither referred to together nor could they be separated.) Now I keep all A4-sized white waste paper which has not been folded or creased, from my own word-processor and from my husband's office. I cut the A4 sheets in half, and use them by the stack. I have no qualms about putting just one sentence, even one word, on each sheet as they are technically waste! But the smooth white surface is still pleasant to use.

(a) Across the top of the sheet I write the topic (of the *section* of the article, not the article itself) in capitals.

(b) Then I write the note. If I copy it exactly I enclose it in quotation marks. That way I know whether I can use it as a quotation, or whether I have already paraphrased the material. I never put more than one sentence to a sheet. Incidentally major quotations (more than a paragraph or so) should not be used without the permission of the author and/or publisher. If you leave out some material from the quote take care that it does not alter the sense, and mark the deletion with an ellipsis (. . .).

(c) Near the foot of the sheet I put the complete source: if it is from a journal, I write the name of the author, the title of the article and journal, and the date or volume number, and the page; if it is from a book I write the name of the author, the title of the book, the publishing company, the number of the edition, where it was published and what date, and the page where the quote/information was found. It is essential that you can produce the authority if questioned by an editor or a doubting reader.

(d) At the bottom I write the name of the library, the exact address of the government department or private company, etc., also the reference number of the publication and its exact location (that is, in what room and on what shelf the publication can be found). Sometimes it is worthwhile to note the name of a helpful staff-member, particularly from a private library or government department. This makes requests for more information for this article, or another, very much easier. To cut time, on subsequent notes from the same source I use only the surname of the author and a significant word from the title, and the name of the library or office. In the back of my diary I key these abbreviations to the full name of the authors and publications just in case my notes are misplaced. However, all these precautions are not necessary for a short article with few reference notes.

- Become fanatical about accuracy. Always write clearly, or print, names of people and places, being careful to specify where capital letters are used in names like MacKenzie and de Veer. It is essential that you make no mistake in spelling. Imagine how irritating and time-consuming it would be when typing up your article if you were unsure of just one letter in a name and had to travel miles to check it. Double-check dates as you copy them down. Be very careful about such things as whether a country town is in fact a city, whether an area is a shire or a parish, whether a territory is a state or a province.

- In some places you may be permitted to use a tape-recorder; check first. Reading information onto tape is faster, and easier on the muscles of the hand, but it can lead to more mistakes when you transpose into type from your recorded voice. However, if you are rushed for time while researching, it is an alternative worth considering.

- Don't forget films, videos, and other material available in libraries and archives. They sometimes provide more usable information than does print. Study the source carefully; establish whether it is original (for example, a news clipping) or whether it is re-enacted. Well-researched fiction on film will provide authentic atmosphere and details, such as costumes of the place and time, buildings, etc. Note sources of films in much the same way as you do for sources of printed material.

PEOPLE RESEARCH

Interviews supply the life-blood of many articles. Quotations from an authority, whether they be pointed, pithy or pungent, add spice and substance to any story. It makes the human involvement immediately obvious, in a way that is impossible for you to do as the writer, particularly if the words that are used belong unmistakeably to the trade, the science, the profession or the culture of the person quoted.

If you are writing on a technical subject about which you know only a little, always interview at least three experts. Listen to divergent views before you write about the subject.

- When you locate someone who can help with information about your topic, ask for an interview. A letter from your magazine, if you have an assignment, may smooth the way. But remember that the expert has no reason to share information with you. If the expert is kind and agrees to talk to you, it will be as a favour. This is one area where women writers have an advantage; they are sometimes seen by interviewees as less threatening, and may be permitted where men are barred. In some situations, such as mining or heavy industrial sites, the reverse is true.

  All you can do is ask. If an interview *in person* is granted, make a definite appointment, and make sure you arrive on time. Arrange a definite period for the interview, say half-an-hour, and prepare to leave when the time is up. If more time is needed, the interviewee may ask you to stay, or may suggest another appointment. If not, then ask for a further appointment. Two or more short interviews are often more fruitful than one very long interview.

- Go to the interview prepared. This means doing your homework. Find out all you can about your topic, and about the interviewee from all other easily available sources before you present yourself at the interview.

- Present yourself in a manner that blends with your interviewee's environment. Dress in a way that is least threatening. That means wearing business clothes to visit a businessperson or politician; dressing in a slightly less formal manner for university staff or people in the arts; wearing neat casual wear to visit people in their homes or in hospitals, or in the country.

- Decide what you want to learn. This means preparing a list of questions you want answered. But don't close your mind, you may be given information you could never have guessed at. Be alert and appreciative enough to accept any extras graciously. You can decide later how much of it you will use to change the thrust of your article.

- Sit where the interviewee asks you to sit, without demurring. You may be placed in a lower chair so that the interviewee feels superior. It doesn't matter. The interviewee is likely to be more relaxed and talk more freely, and that's what you want, isn't it? Besides, feelings of superiority have nothing to do with you except that they have the good effect of making your interviewee comfortable; you cannot be made to feel inferior without your permission.

- Actively establish rapport. Smile. Show yourself to be warm and human. If you have been looking forward to the interview because of a shared interest, say so. If it is likely to be a difficult interview, acknowledge that, while remaining courteous and respectful.

- Be sensitive as to whether or not you should begin with

chit-chat. Sometimes it relaxes both the interviewer and the interviewee; sometimes it is seen as a waste of time.

- Ask open-ended questions, rather than questions that can be answered by a short 'Yes' or 'No'. Be specific, ask 'How much?', 'How often?', 'How big?' Never ask for an anecdote, but ask questions which will encourage your interviewee to expand and explain, and, if you are lucky, the anecdotes will come. Remember this is an interview, not a two-way conversation. Don't try to match the anecdotes.

- If the interviewee is friendly, listen; if the interviewee is hostile, listen. At all times listen to everything that is said, and observe how it is said. Watch expression and body language. Be sensitive to the feelings and the thoughts behind the words. If there is a silence, don't rush to fill it with another question. Perhaps the interviewee is just about to share a remarkably revealing aspect which you hadn't dared hope for. Show that you are listening, that you are interested.

- Remember that you are there to receive information, not give it. If the interviewee tries to question you don't be led into an argument, shrug it off pleasantly. It is precious interviewing time that is being used up. You are the interviewer. It's your show. Take the lead: ask for the information *you* want.

  Ask your questions clearly so there can be no misunderstanding. If the interviewee does not answer it, rephrase the question and ask it again. It could be the interviewee did not hear or did not understand, you. However, be very careful not to push interviewees further than they are prepared to go. They deserve respect both during the interview and, later, in print.

- Clarify everything. Never take notes of, or tape, something you don't understand. Ask politely for whatever it is to be explained. Admit ignorance. It doesn't demean you. You are a writer, not an expert in whizz-gigs or whatever.

- If you hear a particularly apt statement that could serve as a direct quotation in your finished article, write it down exactly, and tell the interviewee you will be using it in your article. Read it back to make sure you have recorded it exactly. Then make a note that you have obtained permission to use it and have confirmed it. If the atmosphere is friendly this will be sufficient. If it is a hostile interview the interviewee will know that you are looking for damning quotes, and will be wary. In such a case, the interviewee's written confirmation should be sought before you can go to print.

Oddly enough, unsophisticated people, such as elderly neighbours you are interviewing for a nostalgia article, are often the most suspicious about being quoted. Their statements are also likely to be rambling and will need some editing before being used as direct quotations. In that situation it is often better to record the statement verbatim. Later, as you type them up edit those parts you want to use as direct quotations. Don't change the meaning, the spirit, or the language. Just remove the 'umms' and 'aahs', and perhaps shorten the sentences a little in the interests of coherence. Then go back to your sources, or telephone them, and read out the tidied-up versions, asking for confirmation that this is what was said. They will almost never realise that you have removed anything at all. In fact they are likely to say, 'Of course, that's what I said. You took it down when I said it!' Once again, note when and how the interviewee confirmed the quote. Keep in mind that everyone's memory is less than perfect. Check facts from other sources, such as official records.

Sometimes an interviewee will ask to check your manuscript. Avoid showing the whole manuscript if you can. Many interviewees see this as an invitation to alter it. However, it is fair to both of you that the quotations are acknowledged as accurate, so always check them - perhaps by reading the quote over the phone after you have typed up the article. If an interviewee insists on seeing the whole article, either read it out over the phone, or send a copy with a note saying something like, 'For your information. Please let me know before next Monday if you believe any statement relating to your interview to be incorrect, or if you would like to give me further information.' Never commit yourself to changing your manuscript, unless it is patently incorrect, but leave yourself open to suggestions. They may be even better than the original interview.

- Do your best to put a nervous interviewee at ease. Some people relax if they hold something, such as a photograph.

- Be friendly but professional, particularly if you are a woman (if a businessman you are interviewing relaxes and talks about his family, it may be to indicate to you that he is a warm person; if you talk about your family you may be seen principally as a housewife).

- In your article set the interviewee in context: the politician in the office, the old man in his old-fashioned room, the street-kid in a 'squat'. Take notes of the appearance, grooming, mannerisms, expression, clothes, style of speech, jargon, quality of voice, etc., of the interviewee. Observe the objects surrounding the person you are interviewing. Try to get the essence of the person and that particular environment.

- Take *a note-book* or *a tape-recorder*, or both. They aren't strictly necessary. Some writers with phenomenal memories use neither. They simply absorb with total concentration, then write it out straight from memory, checking in the normal way to confirm quotations and statistics.

  If you take notes, a stiff-backed spiral-bound pad is the best to use. Take several pens or pencils. A working knowledge of shorthand is a help, but you can develop your own version of quick writing. You will also learn to edit as you go, skimming out small talk and just capturing the essence.

Write out in full any important statements or statistics, and ask that it be confirmed immediately. Then note that it has been confirmed.

Tape-recorders have some obvious advantages. They record all that is said; they capture the entire quote. While the tape is recording the words, you can be thinking, absorbing and listening. Only use a tape-recorder if you have the interviewee's permission, but reluctant permission is not enough.

Tape-recorders are only an advantage if everyone is comfortable with the act of taping. This includes you. If you are continually checking that the recorder is working (if you are unsure as to its efficiency), then your edginess will show and affect the interviewee. Sometimes an interviewee clams up when faced with a tape-recorder; or worse, decides to become an orator. However, even if the personal elements are all relaxed there are dangers to remember. Tapes have been known to jam, or to go blank. Also, with a rambling interviewee the transposing is tedious and time-consuming. It is vital to have a note-book on your knee even if you trust your tape-recorder utterly; how else can you note a revealing mannerism or reaction? You certainly can't pull out a note-book at a sensitive moment, and the tape only records sounds. Make your own decision. Try both, depending upon the person being interviewed. Some writers won't do an interview without a tape-recorder, some always take notes as well. You'll have to find the method that is best for you and your interviewee.

An alternative I use frequently is to take notes while in the interview, and as soon as I leave the room (and I mean immediately) I record on tape everything I can remember of what happened, what the interviewee did, said, looked like, suggested.

- Interviews can also be conducted *by telephone.* This works very well for contacting a busy specialist who lives in another part of the country. Telephone and ask for the interview, and arrange a convenient time to phone back. It is usually better if you outline the kinds of questions you will be asking. This gives the interviewee time to prepare general answers; you can probe for more details during the main call. As for personal interviews, you should do your homework first. Don't waste time on questions to which you should know the answers.

  Phone calls are also useful to follow up personal interviews, if you want a little more information, or to confirm an important statement, or quote, or to check on the latest statistics if there is a strong news element in the article.

- You can also do your research *by mail.* If you know specifically what expert knowledge or opinion you want, write to whoever can answer your question and ask. Explain why you want it. Remember that you are asking that person to use time for your benefit, so be polite and make the task as easy as possible by enclosing a stamped, self-addressed envelope. It may be worth following up by phone, to make sure you get permission to quote your source by name.

Now your research is complete. Take the information you have gathered and fill the gaps in your article until it says with authority exactly what you wanted it to say.

Put it aside for a little time. You have a couple of tasks to complete before you send the article on its way.

(a) Thank all the people who have helped you. Write brief thank-you notes; promise to send a copy of the published article to people who gave you large chunks of time. You will do this because you are unfailingly courteous in your dealings with people. It has a bonus. If you establish friendly links with your contacts they will probably be happy to help you next time you are writing on a similar subject.

(b) Start a card-index file of helpful contacts, and enter names and addresses under subject headings.

The next logical step with your article is to revise it, rewrite it, edit it, polish it. In other words, get it ready for publication. But you haven't prepared the market-place for it yet. So put the article aside.

See the next chapter on how to approach a magazine editor, to make sure the article is wanted before you send it off. As you become experienced you will take this step before you do the detailed research.

As you write and publish, your confidence will grow. In a few months you will automatically query an editor before you write the article.

I have taught many classes of writing students. They have ranged in ages from an eighteen-year-old, who was also studying journalism at college, to the eighty-year-old widow of an eminent professor of architecture. Writing abilities have varied from people who have already had books published, and several public relations and advertising professionals and full-time journalists, to people like the elderly Chinese businessman who, after half a lifetime in Chinatown, could speak and write only broken English, but what a story he had to tell of his childhood in China in the 1920s. Education levels have spanned graduates from all university faculties including English literature, history, creative writing and communications, and many people who hold Master of Arts degrees from Australian universities and at least one from Cambridge, England, to age-pensioners who left school at fourteen years of age over sixty years ago and who cannot remember the difference between a noun and a verb.

They all listen to my explanation about the advantages of sending a proposal, or a query letter about a proposed article. And they believe me. It is logical, after all. But they nearly all say that they feel unsure about their ability to complete the article until it is roughly in shape. When the article is fully researched and organised on paper, and just awaiting revision, rewriting, a final polish, then they feel able to approach an editor to offer the story.

After as few as one or two published stories, they are then able to follow the recommended course of action. They query the editor of a target magazine as soon as the idea is developed and they know what angle they are going to take - usually after some time spent thinking, but after only preliminary research.

A recommended schedule for developing an article is set out below.

FROM IDEA TO BANK DEPOSIT

1 The birth of the idea, from the first glimmer of the germ of an idea. This stage continues while you think it through thoroughly. You might have carried this idea around for a while, snipped and filed information about it, or discussed it with people more closely involved. Decide on the focus you want. If you know very little about the topic, you may have to do a little preliminary research. Does it interest you enough to spend time on it? Will it interest others? Is the research material available? Is the time right? Has it already had too much exposure?

2 Make market enquiries. This includes checking out whether there are some likely markets for the idea. Could the idea be developed to suit three or four magazines at least? Then narrow it down to the best possible one, and write a query letter to your first-choice editor. Don't do anything more on this idea until you receive a reply. You will have other projects under way simultaneously.

3 Free-write the first draft. The editor has asked to see the article, and you have agreed on a length, an angle, and a date by which you will deliver it. The idea has now been

in your mind for a long time, and new information keeps surfacing. Without spending much time you seem to have gained much related information that you may be able to use. Write the first draft. Just let it flow freely; don't worry about organising it.

4 Further research, interviewing, and collating material.

5 Organise the article, and rewrite it to fit that organisation plan.

6 Revise - rewrite and polish to produce the best prose that you can.

7 Delivery, usually by mail, and often with a hopeful prayer.

8 Payment is sometimes on acceptance, too often on publication, but always with a welcome cheque.

9 Keep accurate records - not only receipts and expenses for taxation purposes but complete records, so that you can chart which kinds of articles are most profitable when payment is related to time expended.

Exercises

1 Locate the research sources you will need for your chosen topic.

2 Do any research necessary for your article. Make sure all the gaps are filled.

3 Locate and visit all the libraries in your area. If possible, visit the state or national library, or large specialist libraries (such as the Mitchell Library in Sydney, with its Australian collection), historical society libraries, university libraries, local council libraries, and others. Establish your reading rights, research rights, borrowing rights, and the libraries' opening times. Try to get some idea of how each library will serve your special interests, and record the details.

8

MARKETING

SEND A QUERY LETTER

The big advantage of non-fiction over fiction is that it is often sold before it is written. If you write an article of over 1000 words, you can usually sell it more easily by sending a query letter first. In the letter you describe what you are going to write about and with what particular angle, and ask whether the editor is interested in buying it.

There are some articles which are better written first, and then marketed. They include:

- All short articles. One of the the main advantages of the query letter is that it saves time as the editor only has to read one page to know what you are proposing. However, for articles under 1000 words, the time-saving element would hardly apply.
- Personal essays, where the style of your writing is overwhelmingly more important than the subject matter.
- Humour. This is very difficult to convey in a query letter. It really has to be read in full.

Most editors will not guarantee to buy work from a query letter, even from a writer whom they know, but often say they would like to see it. So, negotiations begin at this point. The editor is now expecting to receive your article, and will include it in plans for a future issue. When your article is finished, it is assured of a friendly reception and a quick trip to the editor's desk.

Advantages

Your submission ends up on the editor's desk, not in the slush pile (the term for unsolicited submissions).

The editor already has a sense of ownership, which ensures that if your article is acceptable, the magazine will buy it.

You have claimed the topic. The editor, knowing yours is coming, is unlikely to buy another article on the same topic.

You have presented yourself as a professional, by giving the editor the opportunity to consider the query first.

After you have sold one or two articles to the same magazine, the editor may prefer you to telephone your queries. If so, have everything prepared as if in a letter, so you can supply information in the same orderly, organised form.

As well as saving the editor time, you save your own time. If you cannot interest the editor of your first-choice magazine in the proposed article, send it out to your second choice, then your third, until it does evoke interest. Meanwhile, work on other projects.

Responsibilities

Your writing skill is judged by the skill demonstrated in the query letter.

The query letter is a letter of persuasion. It is the means you use to persuade the editor to buy your story. If the letter is not well-crafted, the editor won't ask to see your article.

When the editor responds favourably to your query letter, it is your responsibility to produce what you promised to produce, on time. If it must take longer, advise the editor as early as possible, giving a reasonable explanantion, the best being that more research will lead to a better article.

Be professional and persuasive

The query letter should be very short - no longer than one page. (A sample letter is given on p. 130.)

Address it to a particular editor, by name. Check the staff-list from a recent copy of the magazine, and send it to the features editor, or the non-fiction editor, or, if these names don't appear, to the editor. If the magazine is produced in your own state, phone the publication's office, introduce yourself as a contributor, and ask for the correct name and title to which to submit a proposal about an article. Some editors change jobs frequently.

Write in a tone that is professional, but pleasantly conversational. Be witty if the subject calls for it. Be confident in your ability to produce the article you are offering, but beware of being bombastic. You want this query letter to stand out, so the editor will notice it - because of its competent writing, its perfect presentation, its tone of friendly professionalism, its interesting subject matter and the evidence that you, the writer, know the tastes of the readers of that particular magazine. Avoid at all costs any efforts to have your work noticed by using brightly coloured paper or ink, or way-out typescript, to attract attention, just as you would avoid using an excessively buddy-buddy tone to the editor, or the suggestion that you know better than the editor what the magazine's readers want.

Begin by stating clearly that you are proposing to write an article, and would like to know if the editor is interested. (More than one article from a tentative author has ended up on the letters to the editor page.)

Introduce your topic with flair. Give the title, and use the most attractive bait you have. This will often be your eye-catcher. Grab the attention of the editor, your most important reader, with a thought-provoking theme, an arresting anecdote, a startling statistic, or a quirky quotation.

Briefly outline what you will write in the article, and what angle you will use. Tell just enough to arouse curiosity, and leave the editor with the conviction that you have the ability to satisfy that curiosity. If you envisage the article fitting into a particular section of the magazine, say so.

Say why the magazine's readers will be interested in it, and why this will be an authoritative article. List what authorities you intend to interview, whether you already have, or expect to have, any notable quotes.

Establish your credibility. Give information about your experience in the subject and/or writing. Be truthful, but there is no need to tell the editor if this is the first article you have submitted. It is almost always easier for a beginning writer to sell an article if you have notable experience or qualification in the subject itself; it counterbalances the lack of previously published work. That is why the query letter must be well written - an editor wondering about your writing experience, must be able to see at a glance that you know the subject, and that you *can* write.

State the expected length. If you plan to include a side-bar say so, and for what purpose.

State whether you are able to provide photographs, or other illustrations, maps, etc.

State when the article will be ready for submission (that is, how long it will take to complete after the editor expresses interest in it).

Your letter should have a persuasive, positive and professional *ending*. Be courteous, but don't beg - you are a professional writer, and editors need you.

Type the letter accurately, and *proofread* it. Then put the letter aside for an hour or two, or overnight. Read it aloud, imagining you are the editor looking for new material to please the magazine's readers. If you find a spelling or typing error, or just something that could have been better expressed, make the changes, and then send the letter off confidently.

Phone: 123 4567

Alexander Writer
5/26 Paragraph Avenue
Exclamation Point NSW 2096

3 March 1997

Ms Beatrice Birchase
Features Editor
Community Service Monthly
560 Blimp Street
SYDNEY NSW 2000

Dear Ms Birchase

Did you know that more people fear being called upon to speak in public than fear death? Did you know that the principal reason voluntary and other community bodies have difficulty filling committee positions is their members' fear of having to speak in public?

I propose to write an article, 'Speak with Confidence in Committee', outlining ways in which community committees can help their members with public speaking skills, which will in turn give the organisations a pool of confident members from which to draw their committees.

I have devised a ten-point plan for speaking with confidence which I have shared with five local committees, including the Bombast Shire Council. They are unanimous in support of the plan.

The Mayor of Exclamation Point and the presidents of the other committees who have implemented my plan are happy to give me recommendations and quotes. I will also interview several of the members who undertook the plan.

I believe subscribers to your magazine, as members of community service organisations, will learn from my proposed article how to help their members become more confident and active in their organisations.

I expect the article to run to 1500 words, and I will be able to deliver it to you within three weeks of hearing that you are interested.

Yours sincerely
A. Writer

Paragraph 1
This grabs the editor with an unusual statistic, which links to the magazine's readers, and leads directly to paragraph 2.

Paragraph 2
This paragraph gives the title, and tells the editor what the article is about.

Paragraph 3
My credentials - why I can write the article.

Paragraph 4
The authorities who will give further credibility to my article, supported by quotes, anecdotes and case studies.

Paragraph 5
How the article will help the magazine's readers (why the editor should buy it).

Paragraph 6
How long it will be, and when it will be ready.

If illustrations were needed I would add that I could supply them.

If I have had articles published recently, I may add a sentence detailing the magazines to which I have sold.

The editor is interested!

Meet the agreed deadline, and stick to the agreed word-count. The editor has shown interest in a clearly proposed article. Do not stray from those guidelines. A common complaint by editors is that in the finished article the writer has changed the focus or the length. In either case rejection is likely.

MARKETING TIPS FOR SELLING REGULARLY

Write what magazines want

If you enjoy reading the articles already published in your favourite magazines, then you will probably enjoy writing them. Choose about ten magazines that your style of writing would fit into. Note the way each magazine communicates with the readers: check not only the subject matter, but whether the tone is one of involvement or objectivity; check whether many or few quotes are used, and whether the tone is semi-formal or casual; check for vocabulary and intellectual level. Keep copies of these magazines for reference.

Each magazine editor is a particular potential buyer who is looking for particular ideas written in a particular way for particular readers. Study each magazine until you know the aim of its editor, its image, its readers. Then give each editor *exactly* what is wanted.

If this idea of using a market plan seems cold and commercial to you, then it is likely to show up in your writing. Concentrating on your readers will keep the warmth and human involvement in your article.

Develop regular customers

When you have sold to one magazine you immediately become a known writer, and your next article will be easier to sell to that magazine. Do not let your standards, your meticulous revising and rewriting, slip. You are aiming for a recognised position where, as long as you send material which is suited to that magazine, the editor will happily buy it.

If you send articles regularly to a particular magazine, you will become one of the writers that the editor with an idea for a story will think of, and you may be given an assignment. To develop such a relationship, try always to have an article for the magazine in the pipeline. Ways to keep involved will present themselves. When an editor replies favourably about your proposal, perhaps by phone, briefly mention one or two other ideas you have. Tell the editor why you think they would suit the magazine's readers, and ask if you can send a query letter. The editor may ask to see one or other, or both, of the proposals in writing. Send those proposals immediately, with a covering letter mentioning the phone conversation. Sometimes the editor might say to skip the query letter and just to send the completed article in. Don't let anything interrupt your schedule for submitting your first article on time; then work on the second one. When you send it, mention the phone call in your covering letter.

When submitting a completed article, whether it is in response to a request or whether it is a short article that did not need a query letter, divide the covering letter into two parts: the first part will deal with the article and with you as the writer; the second part should put forward two or three other ideas, with the suggestion that if the editor is interested you could send a page-length proposal giving more detail.

Do not become dependent on one market, however. Magazines fold; editors move. When you have established yourself in one market, begin a similar plan in another market, and another, and another.

Most successful freelance writers write regularly for a few markets. There are many advantages. You get to know the editors, and more importantly, they get to know you, and to trust you as a reliable writer.

You might try selling your work to the several general-interest magazines that you regularly buy for your own personal enjoyment, or you may choose to write for a variety of markets - perhaps one general-interest magazine (where you hope to have one article in each monthly issue), a travel magazine, an occasional piece in a trade magazine in your area of interest, and maybe an occasional article in the local newspaper.

Develop a marketing plan

A professional attitude to marketing your work will enable you to sell your writing regularly. Think of it as a challenge.

Develop a sense of the market-place. Keep up-to-date - read current newspapers, magazines, journals, books; be aware of what readers want to read today, and learn to guess what they may want to read tomorrow.

Keep yourself attuned to notice topics featured on the covers of target magazines, and which sell the magazine, and perennial topics which surface again and again. Go through old copies of your favourite magazines. (You do keep stacks of them in the garage or spare room, don't you?) Note what topics are dealt with regularly.

A generalist or a specialist?

There are advantages in being both. If you have some highly specialised qualification (as did the young marine biologist I mentioned earlier who was doing an academic study on the voices of underwater creatures), then your expertise, couched in language to suit the general reader, could be highly marketable.

Even without an unusual and marketable specialty, it is a good idea to write more than one article on the same general subject. Your knowledge of the subject, and your research, can be re-used many times by writing in the same general area.

Probably what works best is for you to think in terms of your broad interests. Most of us have twenty or thirty broad subjects about which we know quite a lot. In these subjects we would have to do very little background research. Range around those interests to find topics, and points to make about those topics. This leads to a situation where you become a specialist in several fields.

- Keep files on all the subjects in which you are interested, continually adding any new ideas or clippings from magazines or newspapers. When you feel it is time to add another subject to your list, you will be able to start the first few articles at least without doing too much outside research.

- You may be asked to do a regular column.

- If your articles or essays have a common theme, it may be possible to combine them into a book.

Double your money

- You could sell the same article twice or more. When you sell your article to a magazine, you sell the rights for it to be published once. This means that, after it has been published, you can sell it again and again. It is essential, of course, that you tell the second potential buyer where and when it was previously published. Choose, for the second sale, a magazine with a different readership.

- Most Australian and New Zealand magazines are distributed nationwide. If you sell to one of them you could still re-sell the article to a magazine in New Zealand / Australia or in Singapore, South Africa, the UK, the USA, Canada, or any other English-speaking country. Be aware that some Australian magazines (eg *The Australian Woman's Weekly*) are widely distributed in New Zealand and Singapore.

- If you sold your article first to a bee-keepers' magazine, then a few months later you could offer it unaltered to the monthly journal of the nursing profession or to a magazine for serious fishermen or any magazine unlikely to have an overlapping readership.

- Australian newspapers, except for the *Australian* and the *Financial Review* are mostly sold only in their own state. This means you could sell your article first to a Sydney daily, then to a Melbourne-based one, and so on.

- Syndication is another possibility. This is an arrangement whereby an agency undertakes to sell your work for around 50 per cent commission. As a syndicated item it sells much more cheaply. But it is often sold many times over. There are only a few syndication agencies in Australia. Most multiple-selling is done by the writers themselves. If you want to try syndicating your own work, look in your local Yellow Pages, or enquire from your local journalists' and authors' associations.

- After a year or so, you could also re-write the article, add up-to-date research, and slant it to another general-interest magazine in Australia, New Zealand or other English-speaking countries.

- Some editors ask for all rights, that is, they become the owners of your work. This is unreasonable, but if the price is right, consider it. You probably will be able to do more or different research and write a much better article in a year's time. (There is more on copyright in Chapter 11.)

Marketing guides

The information in these guides is often out of date by the time they reach bookshops, and they do not give you the *feel* of the advertised markets. However, they are useful to locate trade magazines and journals not available in bookshops and news-agencies. They also list overseas markets, which you can approach after you have sold the article locally.

Check your local bookshop to see which marketing guides are available. The best-known is *The Writers & Photographers' Marketing Guide*. This is published in Melbourne, and thoroughly covers Australian and New Zealand newspaper, magazine and journal markets. It gives a few English markets and lists Australian and English book publishers, and gives information about radio and television markets.

Exercise

1 If your story is not a personal essay, humour, nostalgia or other type where saleability depends almost wholly on the individual style, and if it is of more than 1000 words, write a query letter to the editor of your chosen magazine.

9

ILLUSTRATIONS

Many articles do not need illustrations at all. For some articles, particularly humourous ones, the magazine's own artists draw the accompanying illustrations or cartoons. If your article must be illustrated by a diagram or graph, be sure you can present it ready to be printed, or confirm that a rough diagram, to be used as a guide for the magazine's own illustrator, is acceptable.

SELL PROSE AND PICTURES AS A PACKAGE

You will have noticed, during your survey of magazines, that many articles in general-interest publications (especially travel articles) are accompanied by photographs.

Some of these photographs are obtained from photo-libraries or picture researchers; look them up in the yellow pages of your phone book. Some freelance writers have professional photographers as partners, or they hire photographers separately for each job. Some photos are supplied free of charge from tourist offices and other such organisations. Photos accompanying staff-written articles are usually taken by staff photographers, but most photos accompanying articles are taken and supplied by the writers.

A submission containing a story and accompanying illustrations form a package – a much more attractive proposition for an editor than if the editor has to commission the illustrations separately. If the pictures are particularly good, a package is often bought even if the article is not quite up to the editor's expectations.

Photographs are almost always paid for separately, over and above the payment per word for your article.

Competent and experienced photographers can skip the next section, which is for those people who, like me, develop amnesia when faced with the technical jargon associated with shutter-speed and F-stops, and who need to reread the instructions on loading and unloading film after fifteen years' (albeit intermittent) experience of taking photographs.

TIPS FOR TECHNICAL AMNESIACS

- Take a course in elementary photography at your local evening college. Repeat as necessary.

- Don't invite mental blocks or blind panic by trying to take complicated photographs. Most good photographs are simple.

- Don't think of yourself as trying to be a photographer. Just accept the fact that it is sensible for you to provide the photos to illustrate your story.

- Buy the simplest and best fully automatic 35 mm camera that suits your budget and your back. I began what I laughingly call my 'professional' photo-taking with a small modern Nikon. I bought the non-automatic sort because I listened to my photography teacher's advice that controlling my own F-stops, etc., would give me much more flexibility, and ultimately better pictures. What it did give me were many wasted shots as I forgot whether to move the stops up or down, and many lost opportunities as I struggled with a patchy memory or a tattered instruction book.

- Carry the instruction book with you *always,* after you have shorn it of everything that is not written in English.

- Interchangeable lenses, while enabling you to take a much wider range of shots, are not strictly necessary. Think of the weight. Do you want to lug around a camera body and three interchangeable lenses? If you have a strong back and the potential to become a really good photographer, then go ahead. An alternative now available is a very small, light automatic camera with an attached lens that can be adjusted.

- I now carry the latest SLR automatic 35mm F70 Nikon with a 24mm to 120mm zoom lens, and built-in-flash. If I want to take black and white I have to take another camera body, but many newspapers now print in colour in their non-news pages, so I usually prefer to use that space for a note-book and tape recorder.

Take good pictures without technology

Successful subject choice

- Know the purpose of the picture. Know what it is you are trying to evoke for the readers.

- Learn to eliminate what you do not want. If you want to show the dhows in an Indian Ocean harbour, frame your photograph carefully to cut out the modern liner moored nearby. Then consider taking one or two photos including the liner to show the contrast, not for this article but for another. These unexpected photos are a bonus. Sometimes they can be sold alone, or to illustrate a short article that you have not yet planned.

- Understand reader identification. One or two people in a picture will attract your readers, but a crowd becomes overwhelming.

- The best photographs are of people doing something. If you want to highlight an inanimate object, then try to include an interesting-looking person nearby; this is often useful to indicate scale (for example, if you are showing the biggest potato grown in Tasmania, show the farmer, his grandmother, or his toddler twins, looking at the potato, and perhaps comparing it with a normal-sized potato). No one can be emotional about a potato, but if at all possible try to catch some emotion (a laugh, a sob, or a sad expression). Remember that you must ask the people first, tell them that you hope the photograph will be published and where, and get their permission.

- Let your photos indicate a sequence of logical steps in your article.

- Remember that your readers are not experiencing what you are experiencing. No matter how evocative, your article will not (nor is it meant to) transfer the whole experience to them. Your readers will not have participated, say, in the thrill of a crocodile hunt in Arnhem Land, nor will they have toasted themselves on Coogee Beach. Though you will try to evoke feelings of participation with your prose, try to make your photos stand alone, or add to your prose, not to support it.

- Take photos also for note-taking purposes, to remind you exactly of how a place or a person looked.

- It is essential to keep a notebook detailing the subject, date, and location of each photo.

Successful composition

Read a few art or photography books, haunt the art galleries near you or talk to an artist-friend, or do anything else which helps you to develop an 'eye' for pleasing composition. It is relatively easy to learn what makes a well-balanced picture.

- Remember the rule of 'thirds'. Have the horizon one-third or two-thirds from the bottom of the picture, not in the middle.
- Do not group unlike things evenly in weight or height, but seek a one-third or two-third ratio between two parts of a picture.
- Framing a view with a tree or a building is effective; an archway or a window can make a formal, even a striking, frame.
- Be careful not to clutter the photograph, either with extra people or extra objects. A jungle is better suggested by a cluster of tree trunks, or a close-up frond of foliage obscuring the sun, than a mass of dense undergrowth with no centre of interest.
- Allowing the forest, the crowd, or the road, to extend beyond the edges of the photo increases the feeling of size.
- Take vertical and horizontal pictures, black and white as well as colour (most magazines prefer transparencies, though some will accept prints). Take some close-ups, some middle-distant, but very few from afar. If your photographs are principally of buildings or other geometric forms, take some full-front, some at a slight angle, some at a sharp angle, some from above (if possible), and some from below.

When you know what you should be seeing through the lens it more than makes up for being all thumbs when it comes to twiddling the right knobs.

Just slightly technical

- Take plenty of photos, at least five times as many as you think you will need. Allow for some to be failures; even expert photographers take some poor shots. You will probably take many, but that doesn't matter as film is cheap compared to your time and the costs of travelling. Be prepared to cull your photos heavily. Throw out the ones that are no good - and don't think of them again. Choose the ones that complement the article you are working on, then put aside the others, well-labelled and dated. Later, think how you may turn them into additional income.

- Look after your film. Keep it cool. Don't leave it in the car glove-box or boot. In the tropics, after leaving an air-conditioned car or hotel-room allow your camera lens to adjust to the outside temperature for half an hour before taking photos, so that the lens does not fog.

- Buy your films where there is a rapid turnover so you can be sure the films will be fresh. If you take photos only infrequently, then between photo-safaris store your unexposed film, tightly wrapped in a plastic bag, in the freezer.

- *Never* allow your film to go through the airport x-ray machines, even if the machines are labelled film-safe. If you smile, and ask for your film or loaded camera to be hand-examined, many carriers will oblige. Qantas staff insist that you take a photo while they watch; be sure to take the photo with the lens down on the table, so you will not have to pay for the processing of what will obviously be a wasted frame.

- As soon as your photographs are developed, identify and label them. Keep a more detailed record in a notebook.

Some things are just too technical for non-technical people

Food photographs for cooking articles are a specialist area and should only be attempted by someone who knows or is prepared to learn and practise the considerable number of tricks and deceptions necessary to produce realistic-looking pictures of mouth-watering food. Magazines usually use a specialist for this sort of work.

Fashion photographs and some interior decoration shots also need the sure hand of the professional.

Portraits for profiles or mini-biographies need an expert. In this case it is often the subject who provides the portrait. Failing that, hire a professional photographer.

Photographs are usually paid for by the size of the published picture. Full-page photos usually need the expertise of a professional photographer.

PICTURES AND CAPTIONS SHOULD *ADD* TO YOUR STORY

- This is your chance to say something more. For example, if your story is really about the efforts of citizens to prevent developers from spoiling the old-time character of their small town, you might illustrate it by:
  (a) a photograph of an evocative section of the town, perhaps including a building of particular significance to the town's history or a house belonging to one of the protestors' ancestors;
  (b) a photograph indicating how the development has spoiled a comparable town – showing what 'your' citizens want to avoid;
  (c) a photograph of an area or monument, such as an old

goldmine or a memorial erected to commemorate the exploits of a pioneer or bushranger, or a very old school-building, which is not directly mentioned in your story, but which should evoke in the reader the feeling that the history of this little town is worth preserving.

- Always provide a caption.
- The captions should not only name or describe the subject matter of the photograph (if it is not self-evident) but should also be written to achieve the purpose of your article, for example, to gain support for the rights of citizens to choose the overall character of their towns.
- Be careful to keep captions concise, or they may be cut by the editor without consulting you.

Exercises

1 Practise your photography. If you feel the need, enrol at a local college for a course in photography.

2 Spend time looking at photographs published in the magazines that you are likely to write for. Pay particular attention to ones that are acknowledged as having been taken by the author of the article.

3 Note the proportion of colour to black and white and the size.

10

POLISHING FOR PRESENTATION

Two thousand years ago Pliny the Younger is reputed to have apologised for writing a long letter to a friend, explaining that he didn't have time to shorten it. Writers who pour out all their ideas and knowledge about a subject in a free creative spirit then have to call on their critical skills (a left-brain activity) to revise, to shape, and to rewrite their work. Excess words are cut out, sentences shortened, transitions and anecdotes are added. Whether to cut, or whether to add, is not really the question. The task at hand now is for you to recognise that the material before you is raw and needs whatever action it takes to turn it into refined, polished writing - the best you can do.

The written word can be more elegant, more precise, more vivid, more memorable than the spoken word, precisely because it can be revised. It can be rewritten. To ignore or skimp this step would be to sacrifice the biggest advantage you, as a writer, have.

You will learn to write with grace and beauty not so much by writing, as by rewriting. In fact many writers recognise this step, of revising, of rewriting, as the very essence of their craft. James Michener, whose output is measured in millions of words or millions of dollars (depending on how you look at it), regards himself as one of this century's great *rewriters*.

Rewriting has to be done. Just how it is done depends on you, your work habits, and your equipment. One thing is certain. It will almost always take longer than you expected, and if you do it carefully, aiming always to get the story as near perfection as possible, the result will be a better story than you dared hope for.

While all writers must write and rewrite in a manner that is right for themselves, it is worthwhile experimenting with how and when you do these two quite separate and quite different tasks.

I know many writers start their day by revising yesterday's work. They use this as a bridge to lead them into the new day's work. If this works for you, no more need be said. We are all individuals. But I wonder if you have considered the risks to your creativity that are caused by starting each creative day by stifling that creativity and calling on the craftsman skills of editing, shaping, rewriting.

It is likely that you are more creative in the morning. If so, then reserve that part of your working day for your free creative writing. Having begun the day creatively by free writing, journal writing, or even channelled writing on your current project, then continue in that vein. Do your writing. Get the ideas, the words, on paper. When you have exhausted your time, or the free flow, then put that aside. Let it rest, until you can view it more objectively.

Now take up yesterday's work to edit, to revise. You will come to it fresh, with a more objective eye, because this morning's creative output stands between you and the creation of the work you are about to shape and polish.

ONE WAY OF REWRITING

Any revision is much easier on a computer or word processor. Rough drafts can quickly be re-ordered, but the fine-tuning, the pondering over this word or that, remains essentially the same whether you work on a manuscript or a screen. It is always better to move from the large sweep to the details. So, the first step is to make sure that the article says what you want it to say.

1 Skim for overall shape

Read your story rapidly by moving your hand quickly down the pages. It will be close to skimming, and although you will miss the details, this technique will enable you to remain detached. With practice you should be able to see if the central theme is clear and you have said what you wanted to say; whether there is unnecessary repetition; whether there are glaring gaps; and if the conclusion is logically reached. Mark large crosses in the margin where anything jolts you as you skim, or if there seems to be anything which doesn't fit.

Now read through your story more slowly, ignoring the finer details but paying attention to those points marked by the crosses. Make whatever alteration that seems necessary, either on the page with lines, circles or arrows, or reposition by 'cutting-and-pasting' or by the use of the Move key on your computer.

Check that the points are in the most dramatic order, and that all the points are supported by solid evidence, convincing examples, etc.

If you have organised the story to improve the shape, note in the margin any remaining gaps that need to be filled. At this point you may also have realised that you have included material that does not fit the overall theme. Remove it, and put it aside. Don't discard it. It could still be used for a side-bar, or even another article.

2 Check for voice and overall slant

Is the voice you are using right for this magazine and its readers, and this subject? Is the slant consistent throughout the article? Are you seeing it from the same viewpoint? Are you aiming it at precisely the same audience? Are you consistent as to your purpose?

For example, you may be writing a travel article for a general magazine aimed at 25- to 35-year-old professional people with a high income and wide and educated interests. If your travel article is aimed at encouraging them to take a Cunard cruise which calls at, say, Taipeh and Hong Kong, keep your focus closely on the cruise.

The Palace Museum in Taipeh probably has the best collection of Chinese art in the world, and discussion of its treasures would be of interest to many of the magazine's readers, as would also the great shopping in Hong Kong for European fashion labels in clothes, jewellery, watches, luggage, etc.

However, if you make these destinations seem more attractive than the cruise you will have your readers planning a direct trip to those cities by air.

3 Check section by section

Are all sections strong? Does each one work? Do they do what you want, convincingly? As you move through the article looking at each part, look again at points marked by crosses, and make whatever further alteration or additions are necessary. If you need to do more research, then do it.

Look at the *title*. Will it catch the readers' attention? Does it fit the mood and tone, as well as the subject matter, of the story? Is it in line with the titles that this magazine has used before?

Read at the *eye-catcher*. Does it grab your attention? Does it promise an interesting read? Does it lead into the main subject matter? or perhaps give a preview of the main thesis?

Does your *thesis* clearly state your message or theme or argument? At this point the reader should know what the article is about.

Do the readers know 'what's in it for them'?

Are your credentials, if in the article itself, included in the smoothest way possible? If this information is not part of the article, would it be better given as a sub-heading, or boxed at the end?

Study the *body*. This is the part where your article stands or falls. Does each point relate strongly to the thesis? Are the points arranged in the best order to provide tension? Look at the supporting evidence. Is it varied (example, anecdote, etc.), and does each piece of evidence support strongly only that point which it is meant to support?

Look at the *conclusion* or *summary*. Does it relate closely to the thesis, and is it logical?

If there is a *close*, is it emotionally satisfying? Does it fulfil the promise made or implied in the eye-catcher or thesis?

4 Show, don't tell

This works in non-fiction, as well as in fiction. Try to avoid great blocks of narrative as a way of informing. In non-fiction it so easily comes over as being 'preachy'. Instead use details, vivid description, anecdotes, and scenes, to build up the picture in the readers' minds and allow them to draw their own conclusions.

5 Enough anecdotes?

Have you used too many anecdotes? There should be enough to provide interest and to give variety of pace, but do not include them if they have no vital role in telling your story.

F. Scott Fitzgerald advised Sheila Graham to tell anecdotes in such a way that readers could 'see' the people she was writing about (Larry W. Phillips (ed.), *F. Scott Fitzgerald on Writing*, Charles Scribner's Sons, New York, 1985, p. 76).

6 Quotations

Quotations are usually more effective if used to indicate opinions, rather than facts. Quotations are useful to introduce another voice; but unless for deliberate contrast they should not interrupt the easy flow of your prose. Acknowledge the quote at the beginning, or break in the middle, or at the end, depending upon which reads better in relation to the rest of your article.

7 Does everything fit the theme?

A well-written story by one of my students on the stately homes of England was spoiled by a reference to Rosenthal china on the breakfast tray. It jarred, and decreased the emphasis she was trying to put on the Englishness of the stately homes.

8 Statistics

Statistics should be easily understood and visualised. Don't write, for example, 5327 hectares and leave it at that. A reader can't visualise that. Unless the article is a technical one, after giving the exact statistics, also describe the area in terms that most readers could visualise, say the area of a well-known park. A television journalist reporting on the clearing of forest lands was no better: he said the lands cleared amounted to 6000 football fields. Can you imagine 6000 football fields? Two football fields, yes. Ten football fields, perhaps. But 6000 football fields?

9 Check paragraph flow

Does each paragraph flow logically from the one before? Each paragraph should hold only one thought, and it should hold a complete thought. But writing is visual, too. If your target magazine uses very narrow columns beware of even medium-length paragraphs; they will appear as long blocks of print.

Transitions are always important. Every transition is not only a bridge that prevents readers from falling into a chasm, but a lure to entice them to the next thought, the next paragraph. Be sure the transitions fill both these purposes, and are varied, so that your readers catch no echo that was not intended.

10 Sentence structure

Most beginning writers try to pack too much into each sentence. Each sentence should relate to only *one* idea. Be aware of the danger of long sentences. Keep your sentences short - most of the time. Some longer sentences provide variety and slow the rhythm when you want it slowed.

Check the movement of your prose. Have you used active voice most of the time?

Check that most of your verbs are *not* of the 'to be' variety. The 'to have' verbs are little better. Use action verbs. Better still, use verbs that match the sense of your story. One of my students, a talented and vivid writer, wrote a story about a rodeo. The descriptive words were great, what I would expect from her, but the verbs were all static - different versions of the verb 'to be'. When she rewrote it, all she changed were the verbs, but it became a different, and much better, story.

On the other hand, don't use verbs like 'hurtled', 'leapt' or 'scurried' if you are describing a walk to the post office.

It is best to keep your subject and verb as close together as possible. Readers will then not have to trace back to see who did what: 'The little dog, which was so badly hurt when the ladder fell down from the wall that it limped along on three legs, yelped with delight when it heard its master whistle.'

Check that your sentences are not all the same pattern.

Beware of orphaned dependent clauses. They are most frequently to be found lurking at the beginning of long sentences.

Check that your pronouns clearly refer to one noun, the right noun.

The last sentence of a paragraph is usually the strongest; the first sentence the next weightiest, so put your most important information in one of those sentences.

Sentences that end with the decided thump of a noun are powerful. A verb or strong adjective also provides a decisive ending.

Above all, make sure your sentences say what you want them to say. A television reporter, describing the hazards of living in northern Queensland, said, 'Right up until 1952, there were still children taken by crocodiles going to school in Mackay.'

If in doubt about any of the checkpoints, refer to Chapter 5.

11 The words

Cut out all unnecessary words. Write short, rather than long. Don't write 'Brian has the ability to do such-and-such', but 'Brian can do such-and-such'.

Read your work aloud, and change anything that you are not comfortable saying aloud.

Check the spelling.

Check the tenses. Do they accurately tell the time sequence? The past perfect 'had', if used for the remote past or a flash-back, does not need to be repeated. Use simple past tense once you have established the time-frame.

For example: 'Years ago Tom had known about gold mines. He had spent his early twenties wandering around the old desert mining camps. That was where he learnt to gamble, to drink. He also learnt to face himself as a man alone.'

The gold mining, gambling, etc., all happened in the distant past. But after establishing that by using the past perfect tense 'had known' and 'had spent' in the first two sentences you can drop into simple past 'learnt' without jerking your reader out of the distant past time-frame.

If you then want to come right up to date, use a transition, such as, to continue this story: 'Even now, after three broken marriages, this self-knowledge did not prevent him from seeking intimate fellowship with people he met.'

Check the adjectives. One strong adjective is enough (for example, 'the stunted tree' is stronger than 'the small, twisted tree'). If you change the noun to an exact noun, you may not need even one adjective.

Check the adverbs. Are they all really necessary?

Delete garbage words like 'just' and 'very', and phrases such as 'It was believed' or 'Needless to say'.

Check each word to see if it is the right word for the job you have asked it to do. If this seems over-fussy, think of Ernest Hemingway who rewrote the ending of *Farewell to Arms* thirty-nine times, in order, so he said, 'to get the words right'.

Be sure you say what you mean. Winston Churchill replied to a memo about 'fighting with the Germans' with a pithy note: 'We do not fight with the Germans. We fight either for or against them.'

Correct punctuation ensures that words and sentences are clearly understood. Make sure it does.

12 Read it aloud - and listen

Go over your article once again, and check whether you have tightened up the story as much as possible. When you are paid by the word it is hard to remember that it is better to cut, to write short. But if you write short and well, your work is more likely to be bought. Later, you may well be paid more per word than if you lazily let weak or useless words clog up your story.

Read your article aloud, and listen carefully and critically. Alter anything which jars your ear or trips your tongue.

Your article is now ready. Even if you spend another ten

hours on it, the improvement would be marginal. It is ready! No one is perfect, and no article is perfect, either. But this one is as good as you can make it at this time.

What is the best way to send your article to the target magazine - that is, so that it has the best chance of acceptance?

SEND IT ON ITS WAY

Present your manuscript in a professional manner to the magazine for which you have written it. Whether the editor knows it or not, you have aimed this article most particularly towards one market.

The package will contain the following.

1 The covering letter

This letter addresses the editor by name. If you don't know it, check a copy of the magazine or telephone the magazine and ask.

If you have not already contacted the magazine about this article, write a short letter telling the editor what the article is about, its title, your writing or subject credentials, and why you think it will be suitable for that magazine's readers. Be pleasant and positive, not servile.

If you have already queried the editor and received an encouraging response, then an even shorter letter is called for. Give the article's title, and mention that the editor wanted to see it. Be friendly and, courteous, and by your tone always suggest that you expect the magazine to buy your article.

2 The cover sheet

This will be attached to the front of the manuscript. Half-way down the page, centred, put the title; under that 'by', and beneath that your name or pseudonym for publication. Below that, say half-way to the bottom of page, on the left put the approximate number of words, and opposite that, on the right, your name, address and telephone number.

Example of cover sheet

SPEAK WITH CONFIDENCE
IN COMMITTEE

by
Alexander Writer

approx.	Alexander Writer
1500 words	5/2 Paragraph Avenue
	Exclamation Point NSW 2096
	Phone: 123 4567

3 The manuscript

Type, or print out, your corrected and polished story using A4 medium-weight white bond paper and a new black ribbon. Pica or elite types are easy to read. If your article is on a computer do not use a dot-matrix printer unless it has a letter-quality output. Laser printers are superb, though expensive; daisy-wheel letter-quality printers are also very good.

Double-space the text. Allow 4 cm at the top and the left-hand side, and 3 cm at bottom and right-hand side.

Do not justify the right-hand margin - it makes the text harder to read, as the regular white spaces between words, to which a reader's eyes have become accustomed, become irregular as the text is stretched to match the page-width.

Do not use capital letters for words such as government, nor for prime minister unless these are used as a title.

Underline words that are to appear in italics.

Number all the pages at the top. At the extreme top left put your name and a significant word from the title to identify it.

For paragraphing indent the text five spaces.

If you are including a side-bar, type it on a separate, numbered page, headed 'Side-bar for (the name of the article)'. Then, under that, give the side-bar its own title.

If using continuous paper in a word processor or computer, carefully separate the sheets and remove the side strips. Your aim is to have your manuscript looking as neat and attractive as possible.

Use a paper slide-type clip to hold pages together. Never staple or pin.

Always keep one copy of your manuscript. You can send a good photocopy and keep your original. Never send a carbon copy.

4 Photographs

Number all your photographs clearly. Use pencil (*not* biro or felt-tipped pens) to write the number on the back of black and white photos; if pencil does not show, stick or tape a label on the back and write on that. Number slides by writing the number on a small adhesive label on the frame.

On a separate sheet, labelled clearly with your name and address, and the title of the article, list the numbers together with the appropriate captions.

For black and white photos, send 5 × 7 inch (12 × 18 cm) or 6 × 8 inch (15 × 20 cm) glossy prints (most photographers still use imperial measurements). Pack the prints, separated by paper, between sheets of corrugated cardboard or bubble pack, and tape the edges securely.

Send original slides. A note that they are original will indicate that you expect them to be sent back to you after use, or you can be explicit: ask that all slides and prints be returned. Send slides in special plastic envelopes available from photography suppliers, or taped between flat cardboard.

5 A stamped, self-addressed envelope

This should be large enough to hold your manuscript and any accompanying photos. For international mail, send international reply coupon, obtainable from the post office.

If the editor has agreed to buy the article or has expressed interest in seeing it this will not be necessary.

6 The package

Up to five sheets, clipped together, can be folded in three and posted in an ordinary long (23 × 11 cm) envelope. Longer articles should be posted flat in an A4-sized envelope. If you are sending photos, buy an appropriately sized padded bag or box from the post office, and mark it 'Photos – do not bend'. Instead of including a stamped self-addressed envelope, send a self-addressed adhesive label with the stamps attached. For overseas mail, instead of stamps enclose an international reply coupon, which you can buy from a post office.

Remain positive. You have done your best, expect to sell it.

If you have not had a reply to your submission, phone or send a short note to enquire whether it has arrived. The time you should allow to elapse before following up in this way depends upon whether your manuscript is going straight to the editor (if you sent a query letter and received at least a 'Yes, I'd like to see it' in reply), or whether it is your first contact with the magazine about this article.

If you sent your article in response to an invitation following a query letter, allow two weeks plus the number of days the mail delivery would take in both directions. If you sent your article in 'cold', then allow an additional four weeks, that is, six weeks, plus the mail delivery time in both directions.

If you ascertain that it has been received but you are given no indication as to whether the magazine is going to publish your article, wait another eight weeks before writing a polite note asking if a decision has been made. If the editor encouraged you to send the article, be careful to point this out.

Do *not* threaten to offer it to another magazine.

If you want to try another market after waiting three months or more, do so. If the second market accepts it, simply write to the first magazine, politely withdrawing your article from sale. This hardly ever happens. Writers usually are so busy with their next projects that they prefer to leave their work with the first magazine than chase it up.

If your article is very topical and you feel interest in it will not last long, telephone the editor to arrange a quick decision.

Exercises

Finish your article. Edit it carefully. Revise and rewrite until you are sure it is the best you can do. Put it aside for a day or more; let it rest. Then look critically at it again. If you are now happy with it, package it carefully, and post it to the editor of the magazine you selected in the exercises to Chapter 2.

This is the last of the set exercises. You have researched the market, chosen a magazine you feel you can write for, you have written the article and rewritten it. And now, you have sent your first article on its way. Next time will be easier, and after that easier still. More importantly, it will be more fun. Good luck!

While the editor is considering your first article, we will look at how to be a successful businessperson and a productive writer.

11

YOU ARE A SMALL BUSINESS

Setting up a business may not be what you had in mind when you made the decision to be a writer. But to be successful, to be a professional, you have to accept that writing, having been written, then has to be sold.

The trappings - business cards, printed stationery, perhaps a post-office box - are easy to organise, and are a good investment. Editors, interviewees, everyone you come in contact with in the pursuit of your business, take you more seriously if you use the trappings they are accustomed to and recognise. Most writers resist at first, but no writer I know who has taken this step has regretted it.

The real change is on 'the inside'; it entails an attitude to yourself and your writing that you may have to work hard at to develop.

You will need to think about some of the following while you are developing a business-like attitude to yourself and your work.

YOUR WRITING IS A BUSINESS

Weigh up each step you take. Is it really leading you towards your goal? Or down a side-track that uses up your time and energy but gets you nowhere?

Should you give your writing away?

Should you write for non-paying markets? The short answer is no. The typesetters and printers are paid, the editors and all the magazine staffs are paid, so why not the writers?

There are no hard-and-fast rules. If the journal or magazine is a prestigious one which will give you recognition as a writer, then that may be of more value to your growing reputation than a few hundred dollars payment.

Sometimes a new magazine will ask for contributions without payment, on the understanding that there is no money yet but, when there is, the writer will be established as a regular contributor and will be paid. Be wary. I once did book reviews on the understanding that after three months the journal would be able to pay. It wasn't. The editor no longer sent me books to review, but presumably entered into a similar arrangement with someone else. At least with book reviews I was allowed to keep the books.

Are you in control of your own income?

As a beginner you have very little control over the fee you are offered for your work. You will be told that you are being paid the standard rate for that market. If you are not happy about the rate, consider the three options open to you.

(a) Accept what you are paid without question.

(b) Try asking for a raise. Don't do this without some research. Establish what the standard local rate is by contacting one of the journalists' or writers' professional associations in your city or state, such as the Media Entertainment and Arts Alliance in your capital city in Australia, the Australian Society of Authors or the New Zealand Society of Authors. Recommended rates for professional freelance journalists are somewhat over $550 per thousand words at the time of publication, however, many popular magazines and specialist journals pay much less – sometimes as low as $100 per thousand words. If you belong to a writers' group, (see appendix 1) members will share their knowledge of the local market.

If you are convinced you are being paid less than your work is worth, and you have already written several articles for that magazine and established a good relationship with the editor, then ask for an increase in your fee. The editor may well agree to pay you a higher rate, or may be facing a cash-flow problem or may not think your writing is worth a higher rate. In this case, look at the third option.

(c) Move on. Explain that you need to be paid more for your time, and stop selling your articles to the low-paying editor. Try to do this in a pleasant businesslike way, without anger or harsh words. It could be that next year that editor will move to a magazine with a higher budget for contributors. Look for a higher-paying market. All this is less traumatic if you have already diversified your markets (see below).

Move out of your comfort-zone

Professional contacts are important, keep extending them. You may be comfortable writing regularly for the editor of your favourite magazine. *Don't* write only for that magazine. The editor may take a promotion to a market which is not right for you, and might be replaced by someone who hates your writing. Spread yourself. Loyalty is great, but for a freelance writer another word for loyalty is vulnerability.

Understand timeliness

Know the editorial lead-time of the magazines you sell to. If it is six months, then submit Christmas material in May, Easter material in September. Suppose that in May you submit three different Christmas-related articles to three magazines, and sell two. Put them all in a folder filed for the following April. In April check that the one that didn't sell is still up-to-date and send it to one of the magazines which bought from you last May. From the two that sold, you may only get a glimmer of an idea to write new articles, or you might be able to revamp them. Add, delete, and generally bring them up-to-date, and send them out in time for this year's Christmas editions.

Invest in equipment

Even if you buy everything to make your office/work-space streamlined, the capital investment is relatively low. If adequate bookshelves, filing-cabinets, a computer and a fast printer, a fax machine and a telephone answering device, allow you to be more productive, then they are worth the investment.

Books, too, are usually cheap. Haunt second-hand bookshops. If a book sparks one good idea that you can use to boost the worth of your article, then that book is worth buying. Even expensive reference books are worth many times their initial cost if you estimate the cost of the time saved in going to the library.

The really expensive investment in the writing business, however, is of your time, your life. This you must spend wisely.

FILING - FINDING IT WHEN YOU WANT IT

As someone once said, it is better not to file than to file and not find. So, the simpler your system is, the better. But material does accumulate, so you must find some system which suits your workplace and the way you work. Files are needed for different aspects of your one-person business of writing. Bills, letters, research notes, newspaper clippings, notes on possible markets, details of interviewees, the best place to have photographs printed, etc., all need to be filed so that you can find them again quickly. However, they don't all need smart, and expensive, bulky steel cabinets.

Business files

Bills, if they are not overdue, should be clearly marked with the due date and then put in a drawer or tray, and dealt with once a month. Or, if it suits you better, they can be put in a concertina file, under the date due.

Letters (except from editors) can be put in another drawer or tray, and dealt with once a week. Letters from editors will usually relate to one article. File it with the article after dealing with it as quickly as you can.

Tax

Keep *everything* relating to expenses (even receipts for taxis to go to interviews, etc.), and income. Mark each item with the date and name of the story to which it related. Books, magazines, and computer software, are also deductible expenses. Bigger investments are usually depreciated over a number of years.

If you have a separate study or workroom you *may* be able to claim a proportion of your rent, heating, lighting, etc., as tax deductions. You need to apply for this right.

I bundle everything relating to expenses and income into a drawer until the end of the tax year. This may not suit you. Some people keep a daily expense sheet and collate expenses incurred for each project. Do what is right for you, but never throw away any evidence of expenses incurred in earning your income.

You may need a tax accountant after you begin earning regularly because the diverse sources of income and the time-lag between expenses and payment do make the tax assessment complicated.

Writing files

Once again a steel cabinet is not always necessary. Some writers with a large spare wall cover it with corkboard and pin on it everything they snip from newspapers, every idea or fleeting thought they get, every anecdote, joke or quote they want to remember and are likely to use.

As they begin working on an idea they just pull everything related to that idea off the board and collate them, and then see what they need to add. I love the idea. With everything visible, nothing would be forgotten and old ideas would spark new ideas. But I have never had enough wall space, and I succumbed early to the lure of convenient and easily organised steel filing-cabinets.

Ideas file

Put into this everything you think of, or snip from newspapers. Initially it is quite sensible to throw everything into a large drawer. Go through the material once a month, and sort it into your subject files. Discard ideas that on a second viewing no longer appeal to you. (See Chapter 2 for details of my method for filing ideas.)

Subject files

You will need a file for every one of your special interests that one day you will want to write about; 50–100 of these is not an unusual number. Sometimes it is necessary to have whole sections in your file drawer with sub-divisions. If your interest is sport, then you would need several files for the different sports, as well as a general file. Similarly, travel would need a file, but so would all the particular regions that you might wish to write on.

Working files

Add to these regularly from your ideas drawer, replenished daily. One day a topic will grab your imagination. It is always better, and more fun, to work on an idea when you are excited about it. Bring all your information on this topic to the front of your filing cabinet, or into a stackable tray on your desk. You may have several of these current files; it depends how many projects you like working on at the same time.

These topics are now in the forefront of your mind. You think about possible research, possible interviews, possible markets, etc. The material on each topic stays in the respective trays or files throughout the time you write the first draft of any of the articles; only when you are actually revising the article do you pull out the file. This way you will have a relatively clear desk with just the one file you are concentrating on open in front of you.

'Work out' files

File a copy of your finished article here until it is sold, together with any letters and notes on any phone calls from the editor. Leave it here until you are paid for it.

'Sold' files

Once you are paid, move all the material on this article to these files. On a cover-sheet for each file note the article's history - whether it was rejected, and by whom; the date it was accepted, and by whom; the date payment was received, the date of publication. If you can obtain a tear-sheet of the article, attach that to your file. A tear-sheet is simply the pages of the magazine on which your article is printed. Some editors routinely send this to you. If they don't, buy a copy yourself, if you can. This bundle, securely fastened or inside an envelope, goes into the Sold files, which are divided into tax years; the payment date indicates in which tax year it should be filed.

On a copy of the manuscript of the article, record where and when it was sold and put this copy into your Subject files. You can then draw on it for other further articles.

Research files

This can be a card index of all the books you have consulted that you are likely to need again. Cross-index under subject as well as author and/or title. On the card put all you know about each book's location (the library, call number, and exactly where it can be found), and for what particular information that book was most helpful.

Photo files

File your photos by subject in labelled boxes. Don't put more than one subject in each box.

Contacts and sources files

Everyone needs a network. If people have been helpful to you once, they will probably help you next time you need them, too. This information should be recorded on cards, cross-indexed under names, and subjects of interest.

EDITORS ARE YOUR CLIENTS

Copyright

Writers own what they have written without any need to register it, until they relinquish the copyright (see chapter 8). When you sell a story, you sell the publisher the right to print it once. Australian newspapers (except the two nationals) want first publishing rights in their own state; magazines buy first Australian or Australasian publishing rights. New Zealand newspapers want only the rights to publish first in their distribution area, and magazines usually buy first New Zealand publishing rights.

Multiple sales

Once the magazine has run your story, you can sell it anywhere else you like. You would tell any subsequent buyer where and when it has already been printed. It is not likely that a magazine with a readership which overlapped your first market would buy it.

Some newspapers and magazines ask for full rights. They are usually prepared to pay a much higher price for these rights, as they intend to reprint the article in their subsidiary publications. If you agree to sell, you have no further selling right to the material, so don't relinquish all rights if you have plans to include it in a book on the subject. However, even after purchasing full rights, some publications are happy to reassign the rights to you after they have used the material. You would need to request this, if you wished to use the material in a book. The Australian Society of Authors or the Copyright Council in Sydney or the New Zealand Copyright Council should be consulted for further information. In other countries, enquire from your writers' group or the editor of the daily paper as to who fills a comparable advisory function.

For additional information about copyright, consult texts written to clarify this subject with special application to writers' needs in understanding the relevant laws in your country. For Australians, I recommend Geoffrey Sawer's *A Guide to Australian Law for Journalists, Authors, Printers and Publishers*, 3rd edn, MUP, 1984, and Colin Golvan's two books: *Words & Law*, Penguin, 1989, and *Writers and the Law* (with Michael McDonald), Law Book Co., 1986.

Payment on purchase - or not

This is the best method, but many Australian magazines think it is good business practice to purchase your story in March, publish it in July, and send you a cheque for it in August. If you began writing the article in October the year before, queried the editor in November, had the editor's expression of interest in December, and sent in your completed article in January, you have waited ten months since starting work on the project, and five months since you sold your article to the magazine, to be paid. Freelance writers must cope with these very long delays in payment. When you find a magazine which likes your work and pays reasonable rates on purchase, cherish the editor.

For more efficient control of your business income, seek out magazines which pay on purchase. If you have written frequently for a 'pay on publication' magazine, and have a good relationship with the editor, point out the unfairness of the system and ask in future to be paid when the decision is made to purchase. You will have a much stronger case if the editor has already asked you to do work on assignment, and this is likely to happen if you have established yourself as a specialist.

If thirty days have passed since the publication of your story and you still have not been paid, phone the editor about your payment. If two weeks later you still haven't received it, phone the accounts department of the magazine. If then you do not receive prompt payment, let your writers' organisation know about it, and tell all your writing friends. Ask the organisation to write a letter to the slack publication on your behalf. If this action brings no result consider the Small Claims Court or other inexpensive legal action.

SET FINANCIAL GOALS

Work out how much you need to earn from writing to justify the time you spend at it. Don't overlook the necessary training time (the educational years where earning is subsidiary to learning your craft), but make some reasonable plan for what seems to you to be a reasonable return.

If you have yet to sell your first article, then for the next one or two years you should be more intent on accumulating writing skills than income. Fortunately, writing is a craft that you learn by doing, rather than as an academic discipline. During this first year or two you will earn a little. At this point, perhaps it would be more sensible, and more productive in the long run, for you to explore different kinds of writing. See what you enjoy best, but also see what gives you the best return for each hour spent. It is no accident that most historians (whose hours spent researching vastly outweigh the hours spent writing) are academics on salaries. Their writing, no matter how popular, can hardly ever be prolific enough to give them an adequate income.

Any freelance writer's income fluctuates widely. You have to look at your work and your income through a wide-angled lens.

Part-time freelancing - after work or after retirement, or just to add spice to a life spent raising a family or a herd of cattle - will be more satisfying if conducted in a businesslike manner.

If you write and sell, say, one story a month, that will earn you at least $200 a month, and this can be increased as your skill increases. If you are working towards a full-time career in writing, this part-time work serves as a painless apprenticeship. After a year or so you will know the market. Keep good records, not only of money earned, but of time spent. You may be quite happy to earn $200 a month while learning your craft. Plan to raise that to, say, $500 per month, as you enter your second year. This increase would be better pay for a better article. You could still be writing only one article per month while you work at another job.

After two years, if you want to eventually write full-time, and expect to earn a living income, you will have to make definite plans to increase your income. Certainly your rate per article may continue to rise, as you write for better-paying markets. But you would also think about increasing your output. Perhaps you will change your working life, start working only part-time for wages, and try to lift your writing income to $1000 a month. This will mean at least two $500 articles a month, or more of the lower-paid ones. At this point you may need to start using the same material (and the same research), reworking it to sell a second and a third time.

You should also be keeping a strict businesslike track of your time as well as your articles. Work out which articles pay best in relation to the time spent. It may be that the heavily-researched articles in well-paying magazines are *not* the most rewarding in terms of income per hour. But always keep in mind that you are writing because you enjoy it, so write what you enjoy writing.

You may decide that you need to raise your income to an average of $3000 a month (writers don't get paid holidays) before you can rely wholly on your writing income. This would mean selling six articles at $500 each per month, or fewer better-paid stories. You could also add other writing-related income-earners. This may seem impossible to you at the moment, but keep it in mind for the future, when you have multiple sales, and maybe a non-fiction book whose royalties can add to the total.

At the moment, the important thing to realise is that if you want to earn a certain amount, then you have to organise your time and your output in such a way as to make it possible.

EVERY PROJECT MUST PAY ITS OWN WAY

Experience will enable you to estimate approximately how long each part of each project will take. It will vary tremendously for different kinds of articles. You should also know how much you need to earn for every hour spent. Possible ways to divide up the work for estimating time and cost could be:

- Thinking, the first draft.
- Initial research, permission for interviews, etc.
- Writing the query letter.
- Research, interview and travel time.
- Photography and travel time.

- Writing time.

- Rewriting time.

- Packaging and mailing.

If you spend forty hours on an article that pays only $200, then you are working for $5 per hour. But there are ways you can make the total project yield more. After it has been sold and printed, see what other market would be interested. Delete some material which suited only your first market, do a little more research (perhaps there is unused material still in your files), and rewrite to suit the new market. Sometimes it is possible to do this several times, always selling quite different articles that have resulted from your knowledge and research from the first article.

The time spent on the subsequent articles will be much less. If you sell three more articles at $200 each, after spending only five extra hours on each one, then you can see that your project becomes much more profitable.

There are other ways to add to your income if you are a writer. You can sell your writing skills directly in ways such as freelancing for an advertising agency; producing company brochures; producing newsletters for small companies, community bodies, churches, etc.; editorial services for businesses, other writers, etc.; radio talks; local newspaper columns/advertising; and so on.

For any of this work you may be offered a job for a fixed price, or you may be asked to quote. Be ready to estimate how many hours the job is likely to take, allow yourself a reasonable rate per hour, and then give a quote for the total job. You may lose a little if you underestimate, but your clients will remain your friends if they know what they have to pay right from the start. With experience you will not only be able to estimate more accurately but you will be able to do the work more quickly and efficiently.

YOU COULD WRITE A BOOK

If your subject is multi-faceted and of wide general interest, you could plan to write a series of articles linked in their subject matter and their style. These may be published initially in the same journal or magazine, or could appear first in several different ones with a similar readership. After publishing perhaps ten of the articles, you could approach a book publisher. If you have established a reputation as a specialist writer in this field, it would be sensible to choose your topic with this plan in mind. If ten chapters were not enough for the book you could publish further articles and give the book advance publicity by noting, with each subsequent article, that a book was in the process of being prepared for publication.

DREAM FIRST, THEN SET GOALS

In the next chapter we will look at your creative goals, and how to become a more productive writer. Meanwhile, spend some time thinking about what you want your income from writing to be in seven years' time.

It is sensible to think about shorter-range goals, too. What can you do this year to make sure you are earning what you want to earn in seven years? For now, try breaking it into three time-spans. If this helps, I know you will come back to it, again and again.

One year's time

Set a specific goal for the amount you want to earn from your writing in the next twelve months. Be as specific as you can about the steps you must take to reach that goal. Work out how many stories you will need to write and sell, but be realistic about the likelihood of being able to do this many. This is a goal-setting exercise, designed to help you take the next step, not a task to make your life a burden. Write down the details.

Two years' time

Do exactly the same, but take into account that you will be more experienced. Remember to consider changes in your circumstances: perhaps it just happens that in this second year you will have more time for writing; but it may be that you will have less. Make allowances for what you think will happen. Work out not only how much you wish to earn that second year, but the steps you will need to take to achieve that income. Again, write down all the details.

Seven years' time

Planning for this time-scale is dream-stuff. But it is not entirely castles in the air! It will do no harm to plan from a financial point of view, in a broad way, what you would like to be doing. Think about the things you need to do over the following five years to increase your income from writing. Neither the dreams, or, indeed the steps to the goals, should stay static. Your dreams will change, and so will you. Guideposts are meant to guide you to success, they don't have a chain to tether you by.

12

BECOMING A PRODUCTIVE WRITER

You have now sent your first story out with every hope that it will be bought and paid for. You have taken your first step into the world of professional writing. That first step, even following the procedure in this book as you went, was the hardest. The next step, and the next step, will be easier.

DOING THE WRITING

Developing relaxed self-confidence is essential if you are to produce publishable writing regularly and often. If at first you feel your confidence is less than solid, less than convincing, *bluff* yourself. It is like the old self-confidence trick of smiling in the dark to pretend that you are not afraid. Bluffing yourself in this way works, so assume an air of confident self-assurance until it comes naturally.

If possible, have a working room of your own (a study or a writing-room), with a door that shuts. Psychologically this is a great help to being yourself, and to writing freely, without inhibition. Knowing that what you write is not going to be seen by anyone else allows you absolute freedom to write what you like - and, if it doesn't work, to throw it into your waste-paper basket!

It makes the physical work of writing easier, too, if you have a large desk, and space for your files, reference books, paper, equipment, typewriter, etc.

If you don't have a separate room, set up a writing area, perhaps in your bedroom. Even a large walk-in wardrobe can function as a work area if it is wide and deep enough to hold two two-drawer filing cabinets far enough apart to create a comfortable knee-hole; a slab of chipboard across the top of the filing cabinets makes an adequate desk surface. You can fix narrow shelves on the wall above the desk for books and paper supplies, and hang kitchen-cupboard fittings inside one door to hold correspondence, accounts, stationery, etc. The other door can become an enormous reminder/notice/memo-board for deadlines, meetings, classes, and other writing related dates.

Or you can set up a writing corner that can be screened from the family's general living area - make sure that everyone knows that area is your working-office and your private space.

Even if you like working amid the noise and clutter of the family-room, safe storage for your papers is essential - family telephone messages written on the back of your precious research notes will cause you stress that can be avoided.

Many people find talking easier than writing. If it frees your mind and enables you to be more creative, dictate your rough first-draft story instead of writing it. True, you may have to be your own secretary, and type it up from the tape, but if this produces a better manuscript, why not?

Your writing will improve if you write the kind of work you like to read. So read the best examples you can find of the type of writing you like to write. This doesn't exempt you from diversifying, by reading and writing poetry, short stories, or plays, occasionally. Read widely, but not in your writing time.

Write to make a difference, because you have something to say, something you want to share. Be aware that you are competing for the readers' attention, not only with all other reading matter, with radio and television, but with all other activities, such as going for a swim, or playing scrabble. So it *must* be interesting.

Keep several projects going at the same time. You might be researching one, while you are doing the final polishing of another, or writing a query letter for a third. This has several advantages. If something holds you up – an idea that just won't come into focus, or if you are waiting for research material to arrive by mail – then you can work on another project, instead of becoming anxious while you wait. If you have several projects out with editors, or in the process of being written, then a rejection will be less harrowing. If a manuscript is sent back to you, scan it to see if the story is still as good as you can make it, and not out-dated. Check to see that the paper is still fresh-looking with no dog-eared corners. If there are any, retype those pages. Or perhaps a new cover-sheet is all that is needed. Type a pleasant covering letter, and send it out to your second-choice target market. You can see why the more productive you become, that is the more articles you send out seeking markets, then the less it will hurt you when one of them needs a second chance.

Feel confident that you can handle each job you begin. Concentrate on one step at a time. Don't worry about the next step until you have satisfactorily completed the first. This applies even when, as suggested above, you have several projects on the go at the same time. They are together near your desk; they are together in your subconscious, and maybe in the second row of your consciousness. But as you tackle each task, concentrate solely on that task, on doing it as well as you can, and on getting it finished. By actually only *doing* one thing at a time, you will know that you can do it well. If you have to put it aside before it is finished, note what the next step is. Then push it out of your mind, and tackle the next job with equally single-minded attention.

Steadily do all your work, writing, researching, rewriting (all the steps that are necessary to produce a finished piece of writing). Speed is not as important as stickability. By proceeding steadily onwards you will reach the goal you have set, the completion and sale of the article, and, over a larger time-frame, the yearly goal you have set yourself.

Never throw away an idea that is successful. If it worked once, it may well work again, from a different angle, and for a different market. Keep your notes and write something else about the same subject, adding more and different information, with different photographs. This brings us back to the question of whether to specialise or to be a generalist. Writing of anything and everything, and researching and finding a new market each time, is the hardest way to become an established writer.

If you feel the need for a different kind of stimulation, attend a writing seminar or class each year or so. The to-and-fro with other participants will be a great stimulus to your creativity; you may learn new techniques, and you almost certainly will make at least one new writing friend.

Be aware of all the aches and pains that can come from sitting at a desk, and do sensible things to avoid them:

- Sit as straight as possible on a chair which gives you good support (preferably an ergonomically designed chair), adjusted to the right height.

- Never stay at the desk or keyboard for longer than one hour without moving. At the end of each hour get up and walk around on *tip-toe,* stretching yourself tall as you go. Go to the kitchen for a drink, or high-step or jog to the letter-box.

- Put your phone far enough away from your desk so that when it rings you have to *get up* to answer it. While answering a short call, roll your shoulders and do deep knee-bends. For longer calls, sit on a chair that is significantly lower or higher than your desk chair.

- Similarly, keep your most-used reference books, such as dictionaries, out of reach while you are at the desk. Put them on a low table near a sofa or a pile of cushions. When you have to consult them, do it lounging and stretching like a cat, either on the sofa or on the floor.

- When you stop for a break, run or dance around the house while the kettle boils, then settle into a comfortable chair (like a rocking chair) in a different room or looking through a different window, while you have a drink or a meal.

- If you are in the habit of going for a walk each morning, it is a good idea to consider a change in routine. Early morning or evening walks suit those people who throughout the day work in offices. But writers have more freedom. A short walk at lunchtime and another at the end of the afternoon's work will keep a writer fit. Why not share the walk with a friend who lives nearby?

THE HABIT THAT LEADS TO PRODUCTIVITY

Novelist John Braine has said that a writer is a person who counts words (*Writing a Novel*, McGraw-Hill, 1974, p. 19). These days your computer can count the words, but you still have to write them. You are not a writer if in January you have a wonderful idea for a series of articles that may even lead to a non-fiction book, and at the end of the year that is still all you have - a wonderful idea.

Writing is not just putting words on paper, of course. It is also all those things covered already: thinking, planning, market research, researching, note-taking, interviewing, etc. But all the other aspects of writing, all the planning and research, will not produce anything unless you put the words down on paper.

Plan your work in a sensible way. Working out how long you need for the research, and how long for organising and re-writing, does lead to a steady stream of finished work. It is well-accepted in writing circles that it is not good for your creativity flow if you go for any length of time without writing. But, as you have seen, an orderly plan for any article takes you away from your desk for much of the time. This is another reason why it is a good idea to have more than one project under way at a time: you can be rewriting one, while you are researching another.

Divide each project into bite-sized pieces. If the research is lengthy, divide it up. Then, as you finish each piece, you will have a sense of achievement.

Discipline is a word many of us react against. Instead, call it a writing habit. This is a word with a comforting sound. If you aim to be a full-time writer, develop the habit of writing for a set number of hours each day. The habit is your habit; it must suit you. It may be possible for you to write every day from 9.00 am to 5.00 pm, but for many of us that would be impossible. So, set hours to suit yourself. If you cannot be sure of working a fixed number of hours every day, decide on a certain number of hours each week. If you can work twenty hours a week, divide it into four-hourly stints over five days, or work all day every day until the twenty hours are done, then do the other things in your life for the rest of the week.

Try not to set such a stringent schedule that you will fail to keep it. It is far better to set yourself only one hour each day. Increase it slightly if you consistently want to keep on working when the hour is up. This is far better for your writing, and for you, than weighing yourself down with a burden of guilt when you fail to keep to your own schedule.

My schedule is flexible, and you might work better this way, too. I write for five hours each day during the week, and during those hours I do only the planning, research and writing directly related to my current projects. However, I teach for one or two days each week, and on my teaching days I can only write for two hours. If at the end of any week I find I have worked at my current writing projects for less than twenty hours, I work into the evenings or at weekends. Otherwise, if I work extra time it does not count. In other words, I don't bank up hours. If I have a week off, I have a week off. I don't tell myself it doesn't matter because I worked hard last week. I accept the fact that I like to have several holidays a year, and while I'm holidaying I enjoy it; I don't feel guilty!

The business of writing (reading, and snipping ideas for future use), and the business of business (such as letters), I usually do in the early mornings or in the evenings. This takes another ten or fifteen hours each week. When my teaching hours and the necessary preparation time are added together, I work a normal-to-long working week. But I do not have the hassle of travelling to an office; I can stop to take a phone call from my daughter, or share a cup of coffee with a neighbour. It suits me, and allows me to enjoy my writing and my life.

Don't be hard on yourself. Find the way that is right for you. Try getting up an hour earlier every morning to write. Try it for a fortnight. If this still doesn't feel right for you, try writing for an hour every night before dinner - and having dinner an hour later. Perhaps this will be the answer for you, or maybe writing late at night may work.

If your time is spent in an irregular way, with some busy times and some slow times, it may be better just to fit in a two-hour writing stint three times somewhere in the week, every week.

Don't despair if you are holding down a full-time job, or coping with three pre-schoolers. A writing habit can be developed from as little as an hour a day, or one afternoon a week. Anthony Trollope wrote all his books by writing for two hours every morning before he set off for work at the post office. In more recent times a British lawyer wrote twenty mystery novels, at the rate of one every seven months, during his daily fifty-minute train journey to and from his office.

It is important that following whatever schedule you set yourself makes you feel terrific, not driven. If you have difficulty developing the habit, a few tips might help.

- Go to the 'office' and sign on, telling yourself that you are now working for the writer and that you can't leave, phone your mother or a friend, or do anything else, until the agreed shift has been worked.

- Keep a time-chart on the wall or door of your office. Each day mark the time worked and the project you worked on. This has the additional advantage of showing you how many hours you spent on each project and enables you to estimate an hourly rate. This is especially important if you are considering whether you can afford to give up your other job and become a full-time writer.

- It helps the flow and the habit to write on one of your projects every day. You could allow a proportion of your time for actual writing. Even if the amount written daily is variable, it is a good idea to set a definite weekly goal in finished words. Whether you can write an article a week depends upon the length and difficulty of the kind of work you are doing, as well as the time you have for your habit. But a definite goal of one finished article each week, or one finished article each fortnight or month, is a spur. And when you achieve the goal and send the article on its way, there is the sense of having completed a job, of being a writing writer!

- Experiment to find the best writing time for *you*. To be a writer you must not only write, but you must enjoy writing. You chose to do this with your life. If you are not enjoying it, stop, and do something else.

- Set your priorities about the way you use the hours of your day. Look at all your activities. If you must give up something to make time for writing, do it with a glad heart because you choose to.

- Don't wait for inspiration. It comes more often while you are working at putting words down.

- Take a few minutes when you finish one stint of writing, and make a note of what you must do during your next writing time. This will get you off to a flying start next time.

- Go with the flow. If you have a sense of urgency and a bundle of ideas about a new story, work on that while you are excited about it, unless there are pressing reasons why you should finish rewriting the article you nearly finished yesterday. Working when you are fired with enthusiasm is a joy you shouldn't deny youself unless a deadline looms.

DO YOU HAVE TIME TO WRITE?

Think about why you want to write, be very clear about this, because it is your conviction that you do want to write that will enable you happily to plan, and to spend that part of your life writing, instead of doing something else.

You may have to re-organise your life a little.

Make necessary appointments (doctors, appliance service-calls, etc.) either early in the morning or at the end of the day. You may have to insist that you are 'a worker' to get these appointments. For a time I found that I could never make an appointment with my opthalmologist before 9.30 am as I was always told that this was the time of the first appointment. But each time I kept a 9.30 am appointment I had to wait for other patients to come out. I began to wonder if they were left-overs from the night before, and had visions of people sleeping under the surgery table. One day the mystery was solved. I had accidentally left a name-badge from a writing society meeting on my jacket lapel. I came out of the surgery, and, as always, asked for the earliest possible follow-up appointment. The receptionist looked at my name-badge, and said, 'Oh, you work? Well, if you work we'll make an appointment at 8.00 am.' When I make doctors' appointments now I always say I work (well, I do), before asking for an early or late appointment.

Ask your friends and family to phone at a time which is not your writing time. I have never been strong enough to take the phone off the hook, as some writers do. Instead I promise to call back - and do - after I have finished for the day or during my lunch-break. Another solution is an answering machine.

If you wake during the night and can't go back to sleep, get up and start the day early. Never say, 'I couldn't sleep last night'; say instead, 'I was able to get a nice early start this morning.'

Experiment until you find the right length of time for you to spend at a task. If you find that a full day spent on research in the library exhausts you, make a habit of doing library research in half-day stints. The extra travel involved must be balanced against the fact that you can't research efficiently when you are tired, nor will you enjoy it. There is also a perfect length of time for you to stay at the desk or keyboard. Writing is so varied that you can still work at the writing business, just change your tasks. You became a writer because you enjoy writing, make sure you continue to do so.

Set priorities, but not in concrete. Either before you finish, or before you start each day, plan the things that have to be done during the next work period - and put them in order of priority. This way you will avoid the anxious feeling of knowing you have several things that need finishing. Do the one that is on the top of the list, and don't even think of the others until that first-priority task is completed.

Unclutter your office, your home and your life. Clutter takes time to care for. Have around you only things that you love, things that you consider beautiful, or things that serve a useful purpose. Store everything else in the garage. If at the end of a year you haven't missed it, give it away or sell it.

Simplify entertaining. Ask friends around for dessert and coffee, perhaps after a main course in the local restaurant. You will get to know the restaurants which serve inexpensive good food, because you will sometimes eat there - or pick up take-aways as often as your finances, and your inclination, will allow.

Simplify chores. Make them fit your writing life instead of the other way around. Make this test. Does it bother you or anyone else if the chore is left undone? Or left until after you have finished writing for the day? If you use bedmaking, for example, as an exercise break during your working hours, invest in doonas - bedmaking is easier and quicker than with blankets.

Learn to shut doors, on your own or other people's untidiness.

Learn to delegate. Would someone else in the family be happy doing what you have always done?

Take charge of your life. Look carefully at the things you want to do because they are important to you and your family. Dispense with any thing that takes more time than it is worth. Withdraw from organisations which no longer give you pleasure or fill your needs. Drop some of your volunteer activities. Learn to say no. If you find this difficult, ask for time. Calmly decide whether you really want to do it; if not, gather your strength, and say so.

Keep in touch with your non-writing friends by walking with them, taking them with you on a research trip, meeting for a coffee break or lunch near the library where you are doing research, etc.

Write notes to people instead of phoning them (with an invitation, to say thank you, to wish a happy birthday, etc.).

Short-cut your mail-answering time. Perhaps use three bins: one for personal mail (skim through them first before putting them aside); another for mail related to writing (read these carefully, and if they can wait a week, put them aside); the other for household bills, etc. (check to see that they are not overdue and mark the date due in large letters with a felt-tipped pen). Once a week, take an hour to deal with, answer, and file where necessary, all of your mail.

BEING A WRITER

The first step in making yourself a writer is understanding yourself. Are you a doer or a dreamer?

Do you know yourself?

Only doers get things done. But there is a place for dreaming, too. You can learn to manage your dreaming and to turn it into planning, into stepping-stones for future achievements. Anxiety, a common state for dreamers, can also be managed; it can become the driving power that fuels your energy to achieve your dreams. Perhaps the most important thing of all in knowing yourself, is to know your strengths, and to work with those strengths.

What about your weaknesses? What are your three greatest fears, your three greatest obsessions? Write them down. Study them, think about the ways in which they affect your life. No one else need ever know. Certainly you need not share these parts of yourself with your readers. But if you take the trouble to understand yourself thoroughly, then you can decide quite deliberately how you can use your attributes, your fears and weaknesses, as well as your strong points, to benefit your writing career.

Dream up plans that are right for you

Just as it works best to have a regular place for writing, it is also a good idea to have a regular place to go when you are dreaming and planning. Choose a place where you are relaxed and happy and positive-feeling. There you can look at yourself from a distance, see what dreams are possible, and work out how you, the you that you are, can achieve them.

If you are planning to eventually make writing your full-time career, you will need to base your plans solidly on what you know (your present education and knowledge), on what you can learn (planned extra training, experience, etc.), and on your knowledge of yourself.

A little sustained thought will allow you to see whether you have the patient temperament needed for deeply-researched stories, long histories and so on, or whether you need the faster feed-back of short articles, perhaps including light-hearted personal experiences that can be written in one sitting. You will then know whether, as you gain experience, you will move towards non-fiction books, or short regular columns. Perhaps you might also plan to move into fiction.

You will change, so should your plans

Planning is good if it points out a path to follow, but be careful not to make it a cast-iron sentence. You will be a different person in seven years' time. Make sure the plan is right for you now, and be ready to adapt the plan to fit the changing you.

Be positive, but realistic

Aiming too high leads to disappointment, a feeling of failure, and a jolt to your self-confidence. Writers don't need any extra disappointment. Give yourself every chance to boost your self-esteem with regular doses of success - and celebrate each one.

Project a positive image to the world (you really do convince yourself in the process). Allow yourself only one negative statement about your writing, markets, rates of pay, your work, etc., per month! And try to keep that to your nearest-and-dearest or fellow-writers. If you see yourself as successful, that is how you will be seen by others, and their attitude to you will boost your confidence.

Rejections have a positive side, too

All writing hones your craft, increases your skill. Even if your work is rejected, you have improved your expertise by doing it. If you have followed all the suggestions and steps we have looked at in this book, rejections should be uncommon. But nearly all writers have work rejected at some time or other.

Their work is rejected because it was not exactly right at the time an editor looked at it. It may have suddenly become out-of-date; the magazine may have just bought other work on a similar subject; the editor may have been replaced; there are many reasons.

Writing is a solitary occupation

Writing is done alone, at your desk. If you are a full-time freelance writer you will spend most of your waking hours alone. If you are a socially-oriented person, this can mean bouts of loneliness, so you will need to take steps to overcome this.

If you are working full-time in a busy organisation or if you are coping with caring for a large family while at the same time turning out manuscripts, this will not apply to you. A special soul-loneliness may overwhelm some writers - it is a feeling that we can no longer see what is right and what is wrong, no longer recognise what is good and what is bad. We need the *occasional* company of other writers or people interested in writing. It helps to keep a balance, acts as a check that our values remain right for us.

Find the solution that works for you. It could be one of the following.

- Join a professional writers' group that meets, say, once a month. If you are joining to share writing-talk with other writers, ensure that this is what is achieved. If the other members are meeting for social support, to get away from writing for a break, then this group is not for you.

- Maybe a smaller neighbourhood writers' group would work for you. Writing levels and interests could be diverse. But it is essential in this sort of group that you are not all beginners. A pooling of puzzlement is not going to help anyone. For such a group to succeed, everyone must feel they gain something from the meeting.

- Perhaps a fortnightly lunch with a writing friend would work better. You could share your problems and ideas one-to-one, gain support and encouragement, and generally talk shop.
- Or you could arrange to have a writing-partner - someone you phone once or twice each week to swap encouragement and ideas on each other's current work. Total support will need to be shared during the early period of writing. Editing duties could then be shared, too. Limiting the length of the call ensures that it doesn't become social chit-chat.
- Every sale should be a reason for a celebration with your family, or friends, or with your writing connection.

You can do it

Every time you sit down at your desk tell yourself that you are a writer, and that you can do whatever writing task lies before you. It takes a lot of courage and self-confidence to know that what you write will find a buyer, and readers, that it *will* be good. With each success it becomes a little easier to push the bogy of negative feelings away. It can be done, and if you are to become a productive selling writer it must be done - consciously and deliberately.

Some writers find a few minutes of thinking positively about themselves and their work each morning helps them to start cheerfully; some writers pray; some meditate. If such a quiet time calms you and gives you confidence, then let it become part of your day. On the other hand, if jogging around the park or swimming twelve laps of the pool helps, do that.

Living is more important than writing

Do not think you can give up living to write. Unless all your writing is limited to personal essays, articles based on your home life, or drawn from past knowledge, you must move out into the world to write about it.

While studying and writing, you can certainly organise your life around your writing needs. Attend classes and lectures, go to meetings and community gatherings. But you will advance faster and further if you study a range of other subjects, as well as writing. Take an interest in whatever appeals tc you: history, politics, architecture, meteorology, cookery, gardening or flower arranging. They are all part of life, and they will all enrich you as a writer.

You are your most important resource

Be ready to invest in yourself. Buy books, travel, go to the theatre. You are worth the investment. But don't expect to be, or become, perfect, ever. There is no one right way to write. There is the right way for you to write - that way that best expresses what you are.

Remember, while learning to express what you are, to acknowledge the other person's point of view. Remember that from a wheelchair everyone else looks immensely tall - but it only takes an unexpected accident for any of us to view the world from the perspective of a wheelchair.

Freelance is not footloose

Introduce yourself as a writer, *not* as a freelance writer. To many people 'freelance' carries the connotation of irresponsibility. This point is particularly important when you are interviewing business people or civil servants, or anyone else who cannot imagine people actually choosing to work outside a hierarchical organisational structure.

Freelancing is freedom to write or not to write

If you want to spend your life writing, you will be published, and you will be successful. The people who give up have chosen other joys instead. But along with the persistence, the constant surveillance of writing markets, the disappointment when a favourite story doesn't sell first time around, enjoy the benefits - they include writing when you want, and where you want. You can write in a swimsuit on a tropical island if that is what you want - as long as there is a post office nearby.

BEFORE YOU GO TO THE TROPICAL ISLAND, SET GOALS

Spend time thinking about what kind of writer you want to be. Write down your dreams: what you want to achieve as a writer. The Greeks divided their lives into seven-year blocks because they believed we all changed, or were renewed, over that period. There is much to be said for this sort of planning. How you decide to spend this year will affect what you will be doing in seven years' time. You can begin now to think about your long-term goals, and consider ways of reaching those goals by planning logical stepping-stones towards them. Write them down as you did for your financial goals in Chapter 11.

Perhaps:

- You will be an established writer after publishing four books.
- You will have a staff position with a major magazine.
- You will have a popular regular column, while researching and writing history books.
- You will be a top-flight non-fiction writer, writing regularly, in a freelance capacity, for a dozen magazines.

Whatever it is that you dream of being and doing in seven years' time, write it down. That's the first step.

The second step is accepting that the dream can only become reality if you take action to make it come true. This is best done in stages, too.

In the first year work out what you could do in the coming year which would lead you towards achieving your seven-year dream. The steps should be realistic, and specific. Suppose the last of my supposed scenarios matched your dream. Then you could begin now, planning just how many articles you would need to write each month to achieve that goal, what subjects you would concentrate on, and what markets you have in mind. Remain flexible, but stay on course. Realise that writing experience is what you need now.

Plan the steps you would have to take through the years: the things you would need to learn, the things you would have to achieve to get closer to the reality of your goal.

In the seventh year you will only reach this goal if you have kept it before you, adjusting it when your dreams changed, but never losing the way or turning back.

This is your life, and you must spend it the way that is right for you. If you have chosen to write because you love writing, then you must write what is right for you.

Most of this book has discussed ways to please others - your clients, the editors who will buy your work. That was valid. Knowing what editors want doesn't mean you can't be true to yourself. It just means that you must find editors who want to buy the writing that is right for you.

Remember: writing by itself is not living. Live your life with passion, and write to please yourself. If you do, you will be a better writer.

Appendix 1: Writers' organisations

- Services to writers throughout Australia have improved with the development of partly government-funded Writers' Centres. A modest yearly subscription brings the beginning writer a monthly newsletter, notice of seminars and writing workshops, sometimes study space and always advice and information from more experienced writers.

- **NSW Writers' Centre** PO Box 1056, Rozelle NSW 2039 ph 02 9555 9757

- **Booranga Writers' Centre** Charles Sturt University, PO Box 588, Wagga Wagga, NSW, 2678 ph 069 332688

- **New England Writers' Centre** PO Box 1540, Armidale, NSW 2350 ph 067 752356

- **Hunter Region Writers' Centre** PO Box 5276D, Newcastle West, NSW 2302 ph 049 611696

- **Northern Rivers Writers' Centre** PO Box 1111, Lismore, NSW 2480 ph 066 223 599

- **South Coast Writers' Centre** University of Wollongong, Northfield Ave, Wollongong, NSW 2526 ph 042 213867

- **Varuna Writers' Centre** 141 Cascade St, Katoomba, NSW 2780 ph 047 825674

- **Queensland Writers' Centre** PO Box 12059, Brisbane, Q 4002 ph 07 38391243
- **South Australia Writers' Centre** 2nd Floor, 187 Rundle St, Adelaide, SA 5001 ph 08 82237662
- **Victorian Writers' Centre** 156 George St, Fitzroy, Vic 3065, ph 03 94151077
- **The Katherine Susannah Pritchard Centre** 11 York Rd, Greenmount, WA 6056, ph 09 2941872
- **Canberra Centre for Writing** PO Box 1, Belconnen, ACT 2616 ph 06 201 5105
- **Community Writing Program** GPO Box 1774, Darwin, NT 0801 ph 08 89412615

Important writers' organisations are:

- **The Australian Society of Authors** PO Box 1566, Strawberry Hills NSW 2012. A professional writers' organisation, the ASA is a powerful fighter in improving the writer's lot. Phone 02 9318 0877, & toll free 008 257121
- **The New Zealand Society of Authors** PO Box 67013, Mt Eden, Auckland 3, phone 09 6308077, is the primary writers' organisation in New Zealand, and has branches in Wellington, Palmerston North, Dunedin, and Christchurch.
- **The Media Entertainment & Arts Alliance** acts as a trade union in the field of journalism as well as for theatre and screen-writing. Phone 02 9333 0999

- **The Society of Women Writers NSW Inc** meets monthly for workshops and luncheon at the State Library. Contact GPO Box 1388, Sydney NSW 2000

- **The Society of Women Writers Australia** Branches exist in each state which offer similar services to the NSW Society.

- **The Fellowship of Australian Writers** has branches throughout Australia, meetings, workshops, competitions particularly for beginners. Contact GPO Box 3448, Sydney NSW 2000 for address of your nearest branch.

- **The New Zealand Freelance Writers' Association** 29 Grey Street, Martinborough issues a regular newsletter.

- **Many local councils and educational authorities sponsor writing groups.**

Appendix 2: Defamation, slander, libel, and obscenity

The laws which may directly affect you as a writer are those which cover defamation and obscenity.

1 Defamation is used to describe a published work which is detrimental to the reputation or integrity of any person. This sometimes conflicts with a writer's freedom of expression and the readers' rights to information regarding public figures.

A defamatory statement is termed libel if it appears in printed works, works of art or other permanent form. If spoken, the defamatory statement is known as slander, but if broadcast by radio or television it becomes libel. In either case, it is actionable if the person is able to be identified, even if unnamed.

Truth is not necessarily a satisfactory defence against defamation, and writers should be aware that laws in different Australian states vary, as do those in New Zealand. Defamation is usually a civil action, and 'fair comment' is a defence when it can be shown that the matter reported is in the public interest.

Most magazine and newspaper editors are so alert to the danger of legal action that they retain a legal adviser, but this does not absolve the writer from blame, nor indeed from being sued. If you write anything that you feel may be actionable under the obscenity or defamation laws, seek legal advice before publishing.

One would have thought restaurant reviews, as opinion-pieces, were safe, but recently a well-known Sydney reviewer and his newspaper were fined $100 000 for the perceived damage that accrued to a restaurant after an unfavourable review.

2 The laws against obscenity vary even between Australian states, and other countries' laws may be entirely different. An obscene publication is one dealing with sexual or excretory functions that arouse disgust in the reader. Public taste and acceptance – and thus levels of explicitness that arouse disgust – vary from culture to culture, and change over time. Legal action would have regard to current tolerance.

For more information about laws which affect writers in Australia consult the following:

Golvan, Colin. *Words & Law*. Penguin, Ringwood, Vic., 1989.

Golvan, Colin, & McDonald, Michael. *Writers and the Law*. Law Book Company, Sydney, 1986.

Arts Law Centres in every Australian state capital will give free legal advice to writers, but will not pursue legal action. In New Zealand seek advice from the New Zealand Society of Authors.

Further Reading

Read everything that comes your way on the art and craft of writing. These are the books I found particularly interesting and helpful.

BRANDE, Dorothea. *Becoming a Writer*. Macmillan, London, 1983 (first published by Harcourt Brace & Co., 1934).

BROWN, A. & GRANT, A. *The Law of Intellectual Property*. Butterworths, 1989.

BURCHETT, Gordon. *How to Sell More Than 75% of Your Freelance Writing*. Prima Publishing and Communications, Rocklyn Ca, 1990.

BURROWS, J. F. *News Media Law in New Zealand*. 3rd edn. Oxford University Press, 1990.

COOK, Marshall J. *How to Write with the Skill of a Master and the Genius of a Child*. Writers' Digest Books, Cincinnati, Ohio, 1992.

HEFFRON, Jack. *The Best Writing on Writing*. Story Press, Cincinnati, Ohio, 1994.
Writers writing about their work, and includes non-fiction writers.

KILPATRICK, James J. *The Writer's Art*. Andrews, McMeel & Parker Inc., New York, 1984.

MARSDEN, John. *Everything I Know about Writing*. Reed Books, Australia, 1993.
Marsden is a highly successful writer of children's books, and this book is primarily for young people getting started, but every beginning writer can learn from it.

ODIJK, Pamela. *Writing for Money*. The Business Library, Melbourne, 1992.

PARSONS, John. *The New Zealand Writer's Handbook*. Bateman, 1994.

WALLS, R. & HARRIS, N. *The Freelance Bible*. The Journalists Agency, Sydney, 1990.

WITT, Leonard (ed). *The Complete Book of Feature Writing*. Writers' Digest Books, Cincinnati, Ohio, 1991.

Helpful monthly magazines are: the *New Writers' News*, an Australian magazine offering tips on writing, markets, and competitions, available by subscription: A$59 or NZ$68 (including postage) for 12 issues from PO Box 200, Terrigal, NSW 2260 Australia. Two US magazines, *The Writers' Digest* and *The Writer* are available on newstands, and cost approx A$6 each.

Index

Related books from Hale & Iremonger

Australian Guide to Getting Published

SAMANTHA SCHWARZ

You've got a great idea for a book, sent it off to a publisher but got a rejection slip. What went wrong? In an easy-to-read style, Samantha Schwarz, a publisher herself, explains how and why book publishers make their decisions.

For help on:

* Getting content and style right
* Finding the best publisher
* Approaching a publisher
* Dealing with literary agents
* Negotiating a contract
* What you can expect of a publisher
* What a publisher might expect of you – an author.

Informative and full of insights, it answers writers' most commonly-asked questions, and helps you find your way into print.

ISBN 0 86806 579 X, 216x137mm, 136pp, $16.95rrp

Related books from Hale & Iremonger

About Storytelling

A practical guide

HELEN MCKAY & BERICE DUDLEY

'*About Storytelling* is a useful, information-accessible introduction to how do I tell stories, where do I begin.'
DIANE WOLKSTEIN

'Once upon a time' is still one of the most guaranteed attention-getting phrases in our language. Storytelling crosses all boundaries of age and culture. Stories entertain, inspire, instruct and heal. They're as relevant now as ever.

About Storytelling is crammed with hints on developing stories, whether told or read, information on how to find and adapt stories, business matters, and dealing with disasters. It includes a comprehensive resource list.

Whether you're storytelling for fun or a fee, the practical hints will enhance your performance.

ISBN 0 86806 593 5, 216x137mm, 128pp, $16.95rrp